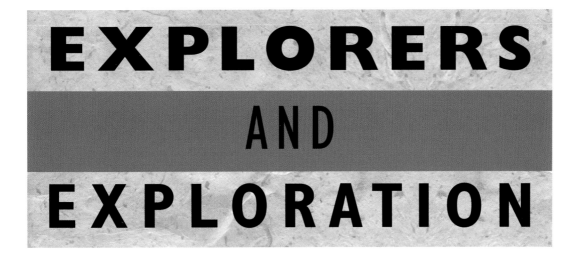

EXPLORERS AND EXPLORATION

SHEPARD, ALAN B., JR. – STRABO

Marshall Cavendish
New York • London • Singapore

Marshall Cavendish
99 White Plains Road
Tarrytown, New York 10591-9001

www.marshallcavendish.com

Consultants: Ralph Ehrenberg, former chief, Geography and Map Division, Library of Congress, Washington, DC; Conrad Heidenreich, former historical geography professor, York University, Toronto; Shane Winser, information officer, Royal Geographical Society, London

Contributing authors: Dale Anderson, Kay Barnham, Peter Chrisp, Richard Dargie, Paul Dowswell, Elizabeth Gogerly, Steven Maddocks, John Malam, Stewart Ross, Shane Winser

MARSHALL CAVENDISH
Editor: Thomas McCarthy
Editorial Director: Paul Bernabeo
Production Manager: Michael Esposito

WHITE-THOMSON PUBLISHING
Editors: Alex Woolf, Steven Maddocks, and Alison Cooper
Design: Ross George and Derek Lee
Cartographer: Peter Bull Design
Picture Research: Glass Onion Pictures
Indexer: Fiona Barr

ISBN 0-7614-7535-4 (set)
ISBN 0-7614-7544-3 (vol. 9)

Printed in China

08 07 06 05 04   5 4 3 2 1

Library of Congress Cataloging-in-Publication Data
Explorers and exploration.
    p. cm.
  Includes bibliographical references (p.   ) and index.
  ISBN 0-7614-7535-4 (set : alk. paper) -- ISBN 0-7614-7536-2 (v. 1) -- ISBN 0-7614-7537-0 (v. 2) -- ISBN 0-7614-7538-9 (v. 3) -- ISBN 0-7614-7539-7 (v. 4) -- ISBN 0-7614-7540-0 (v. 5) -- ISBN 0-7614-7541-9 (v. 6) -- ISBN 0-7614-7542-7 (v. 7) -- ISBN 0-7614-7543-5 (v. 8) -- ISBN 0-7614-7544-3 (v. 9) -- ISBN 0-7614-7545-1 (v. 10) -- ISBN 0-7614-7546-X (v. 11)
  1. Explorers--Encyclopedias. 2. Discoveries in geography--Encyclopedias. I. Marshall Cavendish Corporation. II. Title.
  G80.E95 2005
  910'.92'2--dc22

                              2004048292

ILLUSTRATION CREDITS
AKG London: 647 (Andrea Jemolo), 649, 650, 653, 659, 665, 673, 675 (Keith Collie), 681, 703.

Art Archive: 663 (Doges' Palace, Venice / Dagli Orti).

Bridgeman Art Library: 651 (Index), 654, 655, 660, 661, 662, 666, 668, 669 and 672 (New York Historical Society), 671, 674 (Smithsonian Institution, Washington, DC), 682, 683 (Index), 685, 688, 704, 705 (Index), 706, 707 (Royal Geographical Society), 712 (The Stapleton Collection).

NASA: 644, 645, 646, 676, 677, 679, 680, 691, 692, 693, 694, 696, 697, 698, 701.

Peter Newark's American Pictures: 664.

Royal Geographical Society, London: 648, 652, 656, 657, 658, 686, 709, 710, 711, 713, 715.

Science Photo Library: 678 (U.S. Geological Survey), 689, 690 (NOVOSTI), 695 (NASA), 699 (NASA), 700 (NOVOSTI), 702 (NASA).

Topham Picturepoint: 716, 718.

Cover: David Livingstone's sextant (Bridgeman Art Library).

color key	time period
————	to 500
————	500–1400
————	1400–1850
————	1850–1945
————	1945–2000
————	general articles

CONTENTS

SHEPARD, ALAN B., JR.

ALAN BARTLETT SHEPARD JR. was born on November 18, 1923, in East Derry, New Hampshire. In 1961 he became the first American to fly into space, and ten years later he commanded the *Apollo 14* flight to the moon. He died in 1998.

Below **This photograph of Alan Shepard in a silver pressure suit was taken shortly before his historic flight aboard** *Freedom 7.*

THE ROUTE TO SPACE

Alan B. Shepard Jr. took an early interest in aircraft. As a teenager he worked Saturdays at his local airfield, part of his payment being the opportunity to fly in the airplanes. As soon as he was eligible, he applied for an appointment to the U.S. Naval Academy.

After serving on a naval destroyer in the Pacific during World War II, Shepard began working as a test pilot. As this job involved flying new and experimental aircraft, only the most skilled pilots were chosen for the task. When Shepard was offered the chance to train as an astronaut, he seized the opportunity. He was eventually selected as one of the team of seven men who would take part in the Mercury space program.

PROJECT MERCURY

Project Mercury took place between 1958 and 1963. The project had three objectives: to put a crewed spacecraft into orbit around the earth, to investigate a human's ability to function in space, and to ensure the safe return of astronauts and spacecraft. During Project Mercury a total of twenty crewless and six crewed spacecraft were launched into space.

On May 5, 1961, Shepard became the first U.S. citizen to travel in space—a mere twenty-three days after Yury Gagarin, a Russian cosmonaut, had made the first ever manned space flight. Whereas Gagarin had orbited the earth, Shepard's journey was suborbital (less than a complete orbit). His spacecraft, *Freedom 7,* reached an altitude of 116.5 miles (187.6 km) and flew a distance of 303 miles (488 km) at speeds of up to 5,134 miles per hour (8,266 kph). Shepard's historic flight, lasting fifteen minutes and twenty-eight seconds, concluded when he splashed down in the Atlantic Ocean.

Selecting the Astronauts for Project Mercury

*T*he men chosen by the National Aeronautics and Space Administration (NASA) to train as astronauts were all experienced pilots. In preparation for Project Mercury, they underwent rigorous tests, including X-ray examinations and personality and motivation studies. The candidates' responses to the conditions they would experience during a spaceflight were measured in pressure-suit tests, acceleration tests, vibration tests, and heat tests.

From an original pool of 508 candidates, on April 9, 1959, M. Scott Carpenter, L. Gordon Cooper Jr., John Glenn, Virgil "Gus" Grissom, Walter M. Schirra Jr., Alan B. Shepard Jr., and Donald "Deke" Slayton were named as the best of the best. Of these seven Shepard was chosen to be the first U.S. citizen to journey into space.

Left At 9:34 AM (EST) on May 5, 1961, *Freedom 7*, the first manned U.S. spaceflight, was launched from Cape Canaveral, Florida.

NOVEMBER 18, 1923
Alan B. Shepard Jr. is born in New Hampshire.

1944
Graduates from U.S. Naval Academy; serves on the destroyer *Cogswell*.

1947
Qualifies as a pilot.

1951
Graduates from naval test pilot school.

1959
Is named as one of the Project Mercury astronauts.

MAY 5, 1961
Becomes the first American to journey into space.

1963
Is grounded because of an inner-ear disorder.

1969
Undergoes ear surgery.

JANUARY 31, 1971
Lifts off as commander of *Apollo 14*.

JULY 21, 1998
Dies in Monterey, California.

Above **The official photograph of the *Apollo 14* crew: (from left to right) Stuart A. Roosa, command-module pilot; Alan B. Shepard Jr., mission commander; Edgar D. Mitchell, lunar-module pilot.**

In an interview broadcast on the World Wide Web on February 1, 1991, Shepard, when asked what it took to be an astronaut, gave the following answer:

I think, first of all, you have to be there for the right reason. You have to be there, not for the fame and glory and recognition and being a page in a history book, but you have to be there because you believe your talent and ability can be applied effectively to operation of the spacecraft. Whether you are an astronomer or a life scientist, geophysicist or a pilot, you've got to be there because you believe you are good in your field, and you can contribute, not because you are going to get a lot of fame or whatever when you get back.

FLYING TO THE MOON

After his successful trip into space aboard *Freedom 7*, Shepard suffered a serious setback. In 1963 doctors discovered that he was suffering from an inner-ear disorder that affected his sense of balance. Shepard was banned from taking part in any further spaceflights.

For six years Shepard served as chief of the Astronaut Office, a job that entailed coordinating all activities involving NASA astronauts. Surgery on his ear in 1969 was successful, and two years later he commanded the flight of *Apollo 14* to the moon. The mission was made all the more memorable when a worldwide television audience witnessed Shepard playing golf on the moon's surface.

SEE ALSO

- Gagarin, Yury • Glenn, John • NASA
- Spacecraft • Space Exploration

SHIPBUILDING

THE HISTORY OF SHIPBUILDING dates back to the Neolithic period, or New Stone Age (c. 8000–4000 BCE). Over the course of time, gradual improvements in shipbuilding techniques enabled people to travel farther from home in increasing safety, comfort, and speed. Initially, maritime cultures developed their own particular shipbuilding techniques in isolation, but as cultures came into contact, shipbuilders drew inspiration from one another.

EARLY BOAT BUILDERS

The earliest boat builders made primitive adaptations to buoyant materials. Early European peoples hollowed out logs to make primitive canoes, while peoples of western Asia lashed bundles of reeds together to make rafts. Vase paintings dating from 5000 BCE depict Egyptians traveling the Nile in boats with a single mast and sail and a steering oar astern (at the rear).

Egyptian boats probably inspired the ships of the Phoenicians, perhaps the greatest seafarers of the ancient world. Phoenician galleys, which plied the coasts of the Mediterranean Sea, had rowers on several tiers and were built from cedar grown in Lebanon and Syria.

Chinese and Arab peoples may have developed their shipbuilding skills around the same time as the Egyptians. Both cultures traded in the seas around South Asia and needed ships that could cope with monsoon winds. The slender Arab dhow had a sloping stern, a stout mast, and a large triangular sail. This last feature enabled a pilot to sail almost directly into the wind (a feat not possible with a square-sailed boat). The Chinese junk was a large flat-bottomed vessel with a high stern and a square bow. Less nimble than a dhow, a junk required a large crew to handle up to five huge square sails. In the twelfth century Marco Polo reported junks carrying cargoes of eight hundred tons (725,747 kg).

Left **This wall painting, found in the tomb of the Egyptian sage Ptahhotep, dates from around 2350 BCE and depicts ancient Egyptians traveling the Nile in boats made from bundles of papyrus reeds lashed together.**

KNARR

The Vikings' reputation as fearsome warriors and determined colonizers was founded on their shipbuilding skills. From around 800 CE they developed the long ship, designed for launching surprise attacks on the shallow estuaries of England and France, and the knarr, a wider-bottomed trading vessel. Both ships were powered by large square sails and steered by a single side rudder. In calm weather both could be rowed.

LATEENER

From the eleventh century, during military expeditions to the Holy Land, northern European crusaders traveled into the Mediterranean and saw ships of very different construction from their own. They called the ships lateeners after the Latin (southern European) countries where they were used.

The lateener had a large triangular sail hung diagonally from two yards (wooden poles crossing the mast) that were often longer than the ship itself. This design, similar to that of the dhows that sailed the Indian Ocean, may have been influenced by Arab shipbuilding. Sailing out to sea, the lateener was excellent at tacking (zigzagging into the wind). However, it was difficult to bring about (turn around), as the yards had to be passed over the top of the mast in order to be re-rigged for the return journey.

CLINKER AND CARVEL

The ships of northern Europe were clinker-built. Clinker construction is a technique whereby overlapping planks are riveted to

Below **An Arab dhow sailing in the Persian Gulf.**

c. 8000–4000 BCE
Neolithic people use rafts to cross open water.

c. 2700 BCE
Egyptians use oars and sails to travel along the Nile River.

c. 100 BCE
Chinese invent the rudder.

c. 1000 CE
Viking knarrs cross the North Atlantic.

c. 500–c. 1400
Boats with lateen (triangular) sails are widely used in the Mediterranean.

1450s
Northern European shipbuilders start producing ships with carvel hulls and three masts.

1807
The American Robert Fulton builds the first steamship.

1835
The screw propeller, an alternative to the paddle wheel, is patented.

1840s
The British pioneer the use of iron instead of wood for shipbuilding.

1877
Steel, stronger than iron, is used in the construction of ship hulls .

1902
The French launch the first diesel-powered ship.

1958
The nuclear-powered submarine USS *Nautilus* crosses under the North Polar ice cap.

one another before the whole hull is strengthened with notched wooden ribs. Mediterranean ships, on the other hand, were carvel-built. Planks were fixed to a preconstructed wooden frame, and the gaps were filled with tar-and-fiber caulking to produce a flush surface. A carvel-built hull could be larger than the hull of a clinker-built ship and could support more than one deck. Carvel-built ships required more power, and generally had two lateen (triangular) sails.

Cog

In the late Middle Ages the square-rigged cog was developed in northern Europe. The major innovation in its design was the replacement of a curved sternpost with a straight one. Attached down the center line of the sternpost was a rudder, a much more efficient steering device than the unwieldy steering oars of old.

Caravel

By the beginning of the fifteenth century, the best features of the available ship designs had been combined into the caravel. Built with lateen sails and a stern rudder, these small ships carried a crew of about twenty-five and were ideally suited to the exploration of coastal waters. The caravela redonda was a variant design that used both square and lateen sails.

Left **A model of a Venetian cog, a type of ship used widely in Europe between the thirteenth and sixteenth centuries.**

Between 1420 and 1460 Henry the Navigator sent numerous Portuguese caravels to explore the west coast of Africa. Toward the end of the century, the caravel was the lynchpin of two momentous voyages: those of Christopher Columbus to the Americas (1492) and Vasco da Gama around southern Africa (1497–1498).

NAO

In the sixteenth century larger ships were needed to support the longer voyages being made. Vasco da Gama had demonstrated that only a square-rigged ship could run swiftly enough before the strong prevailing winds found in the open ocean. The Portuguese developed a three-masted, full-rigged ship called the nao. (A slightly larger version was known elsewhere as a carrack.) The fleet of Ferdinand Magellan, who led the first successful circumnavigation of the world (1519–1522), consisted entirely of naos. For the next three centuries the design of all wooden galleons was based on the nao.

FROM WIND TO STEAM

The first Atlantic crossing by a steam-powered ship was made in 1838. To save fuel, many steamships carried sails to use when the winds were favorable and to generate power if the engines broke down. Early steamships were driven by paddle wheels, but around 1840 more-efficient screw propellers were introduced. By 1890 steam was fast replacing sail in commercial shipping, and iron and steel hulls were replacing wooden ones. At the turn of the twentieth century, oil replaced coal, and during World War I diesel came into use.

In the 1940s the first tests were carried out on nuclear-powered ships, which can remain at sea for long periods without refueling. Nuclear-powered icebreakers and submarines are used for modern-day exploration, particularly in the Russian Arctic and the deep oceans of the world.

SEE ALSO

- Cheng Ho • Henry the Navigator
- Ships and Boats • Submersibles

Right **Launched in 1923, the steamship *Columbus* (here shown undergoing repairs in a dry dock at Bremen, in northern Germany) had a steel hull and huge propellers to drive its 32,000 tons (29 million kg) through the water.**

SHIPS AND BOATS

FOR MUCH OF HUMAN HISTORY, the movement of people was restricted by the difficulty of crossing large or unnavigable bodies of water. Watergoing vessels, whether primitive reed rafts, the great wooden galleons of the Age of Discovery, or modern-day nuclear-powered submarines, have played an essential role in the history of exploration. Much more than mere means of transport, ships and boats are as much a part of the story of exploration as the people who travel in them.

Left **A nineteenth-century depiction of one of the most famous fleets in history: the *Pinta, Niña* and *Santa María*, commanded by Christopher Columbus, sailing west from Spain toward the Americas in 1492.**

THE AGE OF DISCOVERY

Between 1419 and 1460 Prince Henry of Portugal (known as Henry the Navigator) oversaw the systematic exploration of the coast of West Africa. His fleets consisted largely of caravels, small wooden ships of around fifty or sixty tons (45,000–54,000 kg) with triangular (lateen) sails and a crew of around twenty-five.

A modified caravel, called the caravela redonda, was the explorer's ship of choice for the next hundred years. Perhaps the most famous was Christopher Columbus's flagship, *Santa María*, which he sailed across the Atlantic in 1492. The caravela redonda was used by Vasco da Gama to reach India (1497–1498) and by Ferdinand Magellan to circumnavigate the globe (1519–1522).

Despite their ability to withstand the rigors of long voyages and to carry large stores of food and water, caravels were remarkably small. Francis Drake's *Golden Hind* weighed only 100 tons (90,718 kg), William Dampier's *Roebuck* less than 300 tons (272,155 kg), and James Cook's *Endeavour* 360 tons (326,587 kg). (By comparison, the *Titanic* weighed 66,000 tons, or almost 60 million kg). Caravels were built small because large ships could easily run aground in uncharted shallow waters, coves, and reefs.

THE DESCENT OF THE AMAZON

On expeditions into the interior of continents, explorers tend to prefer a river route, as distance can be covered much more quickly by water than by land. In 1540 a huge Spanish expedition led by Gonzalo Pizarro marched east across the Andes Mountains from Quito, in northwestern South America. When supplies ran short, the party's only means of survival seemed to be to follow a fast-flowing river, the Napo. The men spent several weeks building a sailing boat, the *San Pedro,* and in April 1541 Francisco de Orellana was ordered to sail downstream, find food, and return. After three days Orellana entered a larger river, and he and his small group of men built a second boat, the *Victoria.* They found food, but the current was too strong to make the return journey. After traveling some three thousand miles (4,750 km), Orellana's party reached the Atlantic on August 26, 1542, having made the first European descent of the Amazon River.

From the mouth of the Amazon, they sailed their two homemade boats north to the Caribbean. (In the meantime, Gonzalo Pizarro and his team had been forced to eat their horses and dogs. Only a few survivors managed to struggle back to Quito.)

SEARCHING FOR ROUTES TO ASIA

From the late fifteenth century, Spain and Portugal dominated the southern oceans. The English and the French began to search for an alternative trade route to the East in northern waters.

In 1497 an English voyage led by John Cabot reached Newfoundland. A number of English and French voyages followed, and penetration into the North American interior was soon under way. A principal motive was the search for a northwest passage, a waterway across or around America that would join the Atlantic and the Pacific. Other northern European explorers hoped to find a northeast passage through the Russian Arctic. Ships searching for both passages were often turned back or even crushed by masses of moving ice. Until well into the eighteenth century, Arctic voyages frequently ended in the loss of all lives.

NATIVE AMERICAN CANOES

Many explorers benefited from using rivergoing craft made by people native to the area being explored. When the first French settlers, led by Samuel de Champlain, arrived in Canada in the early 1600s, they formed trading and military alliances with local Native American groups, particularly the Huron and the Algonquin. Champlain was the first European to conclude that the country could be explored only with the help of native peoples and their boats. Over the years, European explorers and fur traders made a number of adaptations to the size, construction, and carrying capacity of native canoes.

Below **A sixteenth-century copperplate engraving of Magellan's *Victoria*, the first ship to circumnavigate the globe.**

Magellan and the *Victoria*

*I*n October 1518 Ferdinand Magellan took delivery of five battered ships. He was planning to sail to the East Indies (present-day Indonesia) via South America but was short of money—a common predicament for explorers—and the ships were the best he could afford. He spent eighteen months in the shipyards of Seville, in southern Spain, repairing the ships and making them ready for the voyage.

The *Victoria,* the only one of the five ships to survive the voyage, completed the first circumnavigation of the globe. The *Victoria* was a nao of eighty-five tons (77,111 kg) with a crew of forty-two. After returning from the epic voyage, which lasted three years and one month, *Victoria* went on to make three Atlantic crossings. The ship was lost at sea in 1525, on the way back to Europe from Hispaniola (an island in the Caribbean).

Above **A three-masted Dutch sailing ship—the one pictured in this sixteenth-century oil is battling a storm—required a much smaller crew than its English counterpart.**

In 1793 Alexander Mackenzie and his nine companions used a twenty-five-foot (7.6 m) birchbark that could carry three thousand pounds (1,361 kg) of provisions to navigate the Mackenzie River to the Pacific. However, travel by canoe was not without its dangers. In 1805, on the return leg of their pioneering exploration of the American West, Meriwether Lewis and William Clark lost many of the specimens they had collected and records they had made when their canoe capsized.

PACIFIC VOYAGES

After Ferdinand Magellan's historic crossing of the Pacific in 1520 and 1521, a number of European powers launched voyages in the region. Perhaps the most successful were the Dutch, who, in the early seventeenth century,

1419–1460
Henry the Navigator's caravels explore the West African coastline.

1492
Christopher Columbus crosses the Atlantic in the *Santa María.*

1497–1498
Vasco da Gama sails to India by way of the Cape of Good Hope.

1497
John Cabot reaches Newfoundland.

1522
Ferdinand Magellan's *Victoria* returns to Spain after circumnavigating the globe.

1541–1542
Francisco de Orellana makes the first descent of the Amazon River.

1577
Francis Drake sets out with five ships, including the *Golden Hind,* in search of *Terra Australis* (the conjectural southern continent) and the Northwest Passage.

1596–1598
Cornelis and Frederik Houtman establish first Dutch trade contact with the East Indies.

succeeded in wresting control of the East Indies spice trade from the Portuguese.

The account of the Spanish voyage made by Pedro Fernández de Quirós from South America across the Pacific (1605–1606) was widely translated. Among those influenced by Quirós's account was the Frenchman Louis-Antoine de Bougainville, who sailed around the world (1766–1769) aboard the *Boudeuse*. The Englishman Philip Carteret circumnavigated the globe twice between 1764 and 1769. It is remarkable that he survived the Pacific crossing on his second voyage: his ship, the *Swallow*, was totally unsuitable and leaked throughout the journey.

Below **A depiction of the *Endeavour*, James Cook's ship on his first voyage across the Pacific.**

Captain Cook and the *Endeavour*

The ship chosen by the Royal Navy in 1768 for James Cook's first great voyage into the Pacific was the *Endeavour*, a sturdy little coal ship that measured 106 feet (30 m) and had a strong, flat-bottomed hull that was suited to exploration of shallow waters. In the Royal Navy dockyards at Deptford, southeastern London, a new deck and ten cabins were added to accommodate the ninety-seven men on board.

Cook was concerned that he and all of his crew remain healthy and happy. Among the provisions were pickled cabbage, carrot marmalade, and citrus preserves, nutritious foods that he hoped would protect his men from scurvy, a disease that killed a great many sailors and explorers. He used charcoal stoves to provide heating between the decks and introduced a system of watches to ensure his men enjoyed a proper night's sleep. The primary aim of Cook's voyage was scientific investigation; the *Endeavour* was the best-equipped ship that had ever been sent on such a voyage.

1608
Samuel de Champlain establishes a colony on the site of present-day Quebec.

1699–1701
William Dampier surveys the northwestern coast of Australia for the British navy, but his ship *Roebuck* is so rotten that it sinks on the way home.

1768
James Cook sets off in the *Endeavour* on the first of his three voyages across the Pacific.

1887–1889
Nils Adolf Erik Nordenskiöld's steam-powered whaling ship *Vega* makes the first transit of the Northeast Passage.

1905
Roald Amundsen's *Gjøa* completes the first navigation of the Northwest Passage.

1977
The nuclear-powered icebreaker *Artika* reaches the North Pole.

Right **In 1915, when Ernest Shackleton's ship *Endurance* was crushed by ice and sank into Antarctic waters, his men were left stranded with little hope of rescue.**

SHIPS IN THE ANTARCTIC

In 1773, on his second Pacific voyage, James Cook sailed around Antarctica. Although thick pack ice prevented him from seeing or reaching the continent, his exploration of far southern latitudes finally put to rest the long-held view that a great continent existed in southern waters (the so-called *Terra Australis Incognita*, "unknown southern land").

Nevertheless, the southern oceans held other riches. British and American whalers and sealers were already active in the South Atlantic when, in 1819, the Russian Fabian Gottlieb von Bellinghausen led an exploration of the Antarctic. Bellingshausen's flagship, *Vostock* (Russian for "east"), was a six-hundred-ton (544,000 kg) corvette. It was accompanied by a smaller ship, the *Mirny* ("peaceful"). The first ship to spend a winter in the Antarctic, the *Belgica,* was trapped in the ice of the Bellinghausen Sea from 1898 to 1899.

EXPLORING THE PAST

Much of what is known about early ships and boats is the result of the work of marine archaeologists. By exploring and examining shipwrecks and corroborating this evidence with any existing written records, marine archaeologists are able to reconstruct ships of the past. In 1983 researchers at the University of Queensland, in Australia, began studying the *Pandora*, sunk virtually intact after hitting the Great Barrier Reef in 1791. *Pandora* was on a mission to apprehend the *Bounty* mutineers, who had set Captain William Bligh and eighteen others adrift. Nine diving expeditions have been launched to retrieve artifacts from the wreck. It is hoped that such objects will help archaeologists to piece together more information about life on board an eighteenth-century British warship and about the nature of exchanges between the crew and the Pacific islanders they encountered.

The *Discovery*

Discovery, a 172-foot (52.4 m) ice-strengthened wooden sailing ship with auxiliary engines, was built as a research vessel for the 1901–1904 British National Antarctic Expedition, which was led by Robert Falcon Scott. The ship was modeled on a whaler, also called *Discovery*, that had been used in the Arctic in the 1870s and had proved able to cope with large waves. Sloping, iron-shod bows allowed Scott's *Discovery* to ride up onto the ice, and the weight of the ship then brought it smashing down into the water. *Discovery* also had a retractable propeller and rudder that could be protected from ice damage.

Discovery spent two years frozen in the Antarctic ice. At the end of the expedition, Scott was unable to free his ship, and it seemed as if it would have to be abandoned. Eventually Scott succeeded, thanks to his use of explosives and an auspicious change in wind direction.

In 1905 *Discovery* was sold to the Hudson Bay Company (a British fur-trading conglomerate operating in Canada) to be used as a merchant vessel. After World War I, it carried goods between Archangel, in Arctic Russia, and the Black Sea. In 1916 the ship was loaned for the rescue effort of Ernest Shackleton's crew, stranded on Elephant Island in the Antarctic, but the rescue was successfully completed before it arrived. From 1925 to 1927, *Discovery* was used for oceanographic research in the seas between Cape Town (South Africa), Antarctica, and Cape Horn (South America). In 1929 Douglas Mawson used *Discovery* on a combined British, Australian, and New Zealand Antarctic expedition. *Discovery* ended its days as a training ship for boy scouts in London and is now on display in Dundee, Scotland, where it was built.

Below Captain Scott's *Discovery*, pictured frozen in the ice during the 1901–1904 British National Antarctic Expedition.

Above **The icebreaker USS *Atka* looms above the ice-thickened Antarctic waters off McMurdo Station, on the Ross Ice Shelf.**

RECONSTRUCTING ANCIENT SHIPS

Several explorers have tested theories about the ships and boats of the past by reenacting their voyages. In 1947 Thor Heyerdahl, a Norwegian anthropologist, built the *Kon-Tiki,* a balsa wood and bamboo raft, and sailed five thousand miles (8,000 km) from Peru to Polynesia. His voyage supported his theory that the Pacific islands had been colonized by people from South America (and not from Southeast Asia, as was generally believed).

In 1976 Tim Severin, an Englishman, crossed the North Atlantic in a curragh (a wooden-framed boat covered with leather ox hides) named the *Brendan* to test the theory that Irish monks could have reached North America eight hundred years before Columbus did so. In 1984 Severin built the *Argo,* a replica of a twenty-oar Bronze Age galley (of the kind used around 1200 BCE), to re-create the legendary voyage of Jason and the Argonauts.

Hovercraft

Hovercraft are amphibious vehicles (ones suited to land and water travel) that float on cushions of air generated by fans and trapped in a heavy rubber skirt. Hovercraft are used as commercial ferries, as military vehicles, and for exploratory expeditions along rivers and across marshy terrain. The 1969–1970 Trans-Africa Hovercraft made a five-thousand-mile (8,000 km) journey through western and equatorial Africa and proved itself particularly well suited to travel through the reed beds and shallow open water of Lake Chad. It coped well on relatively flat ground and did minimal damage, even passing over small animals and birds' eggs without damaging them, but did not cope well with steep inclines or big waves.

SILK ROAD

ONE OF THE GREAT THOROUGHFARES of the ancient and medieval world, the Silk Road stretched some five thousand miles (8,050 km) from China to the Mediterranean across some of the most hostile terrain in the world. Traveled by merchants and missionaries between the second century BCE and the thirteenth century CE, more often in stages than in its entirety, the Silk Road brought the great civilizations of Europe, India, and China into contact with one other and enabled the exchange not only of silk and other commodities but also of religion, culture, and wisdom.

EAST MEETS WEST

In early history there was very little contact between the people of ancient Greece and those of ancient China, seperated as they were by parched expanses of desert and high snow-capped mountains. In the fourth century BCE Alexander the Great marched west from Greece across Persia to northern India and in the process pioneered a new route south of the Caspian Sea. From the opposite direction, in the second century BCE Zhang Qian (Chang Chi'en), sent by the Chinese emperor on a diplomatic mission to central Asia, forged a route from China across the Gobi Desert.

It is generally thought that the Romans first enountered silk while battling the Parthians (a people who lived around the southeastern shore of the Caspian Sea) sometime during the first century BCE. Traders began to import silk shortly afterward, and by the first century CE silk goods were highly prized commodities among wealthy Romans.

Rarely, if ever, would any single person have traveled the entire length of the Silk Road. Goods bought at one trading post were taken on to the next trading post to be sold again and in this way were passed gradually along the route in stages before they eventually reached the consumers.

Below **This Persian miniature depicts the court of the Ilkhanid dynasty of Mongols, who ruled most of western Asia from 1256 to 1353 and oversaw the Silk Road's busiest and most illustrious era.**

Above **This gigantic rock-carved statue of the Buddha was one of a pair that stood in Bamian, Afghanistan, until they were destroyed in 2001.**

PILGRIM TRAIL

From its early days, the Silk Road facilitated not only the exchange of goods but also the exchange of cultural and religious influence. The route through the Hindu Kush Mountains was an important path for the expansion of Buddhism from India in the fourth and fifth centuries CE and, from the tenth century, for the spread of Islam in the opposite direction.

Buddhism gained many new followers in China. One of them, the monk Faxian, traveled the Silk Route into northern India with the aim of gathering sacred writings from the Buddhist homeland and taking them back to

326 BCE
Alexander the Great enters India along what will become the Silk Road.

138 BCE
Zhang Qian (Chang Ch'ien) begins exploration of the Silk Road from China to Samarkand.

c. 402 CE
Faxian reaches India from China via the Silk Road.

618–907
With the Tang dynasty in power in China, the Silk Road is widely used.

645
Hsüan-tsang returns to China after traveling to southern India.

1246
John of Piano Carpini crosses central Asia to visit the Mongol ruler at Karakorum.

1259
The Mongol king Kublai Khan becomes emperor of China. The Silk Road flourishes.

1275
Marco Polo reaches Beijing.

1368
After the inward-looking Ming dynasty comes to power in China, the Silk Road begins to decline.

1498
Vasco da Gama's sea voyage to India opens up an alternative trade route between Asia and Europe.

1900–1902
Marc Aurel Stein's first expedition to sites along the Silk Road leads to a rediscovery of the ancient trail by archaeologists and tourists.

Samarkand

Samarkand, in eastern central Uzbekistan, is one of the world's most famous cities. Alexander the Great rested there in 328 BCE on his march across central Asia. The Mongol conqueror Genghis Khan looted the city in 1221 CE. At the end of the fourteenth century, the Turkic emperor Timur (known also as Tamerlane or Tamburlaine) rebuilt the city as the capital of his vast empire.

Samarkand derived its importance from its position at a crossroads on the Silk Road. It was said that when the city was at its most magnificent, around the year 1400, Samarkand boasted every race, religion, and commercial product the world possessed. Modern Samarkand remains a thriving city whose legendary past lures many tourists.

China. In 399, when he began his journey, he was already sixty-five. Traveling by camel train, he crossed the Takla Makan Desert, whose rolling sand dunes are up to three hundred feet (90 m) high. The seventeen-day crossing brought Faxian to the oasis now known as Lop Nor. Faxian eventually reached India by way of Kashgar. After he returned to China by sea in 414, his account of his travels greatly enriched Chinese geography.

In the seventh century Hsüan-tsang, another Chinese Buddhist monk in search of Buddhist texts, also made the dangerous journey to India along a northerly route that took him through Tashkent and Samarkand. His account of the sights he saw during his sixteen-year absence gave the Chinese their first reliable information about some of the distant lands through which the Silk Route passed. On his return journey Hsüan-tsang braved the Takla Makan, noting, "There is no road, and travelers in coming and going have only to look for the deserted bones of man and beast as their guide."

Below **The Gur-I-Amir Mausoleum, a Muslim shrine in the central Asian city of Samarkand, was built around 1403. Islam spread east along the Silk Road from central Asia.**

RISE AND FALL

The precious cargoes transported along the Silk Road made those who carried them a prime target for ambush. At times when China was powerful, it could exert firm control over its western provinces and guarantee the safety of travelers. During these periods, trade along the Silk Road thrived. Together with silk, traders exported lacquerware, spices (especially cinnamon), furs, ceramics, and jade from the East. In the opposite direction, glassware, woollen and linen cloth, gold, ivory (gathered by Europeans from Africa and India), coral, pearls, amber, and all kinds of jewels were exported from Europe to China.

When Chinese power was weaker, eastern sections of the Silk Road became too dangerous. The route fell out of use in the fourth century but was restored in the seventh century, a time when the Tang dynasty kept order in western China and the western part of the route was controlled by Muslims. When the Tang dynasty fell in 907, use of the Silk Road declined once again.

MONGOL PEACE

The Silk Road's last era of greatness began with the accession of the Mongol emperors in the thirteenth century. By 1230 Mongol power stretched from the Middle East to China, and under the terms of the so-called *Pax Mongolica* (Mongol peace), the safety of Silk Road travelers was guaranteed.

During the thirteenth century Catholic authorities in Europe wondered whether the Mongols might be a useful ally against their Muslim enemies. In 1246 a Franciscan friar, Giovanni da Pian del Carpini (John of Piano Carpini), traveled along the Silk Road to the court of Kublai Khan (the Mongol king) as an envoy of Pope Innocent IV. He was followed in 1253 by William of Rubruck, also a Franciscan

Below **The secrets of manufacturing silk were closely guarded by the Chinese. This sixteenth-century engraving depicts monks presenting silkworms, smuggled out of China, to Emperor Justinian, the sixth-century ruler of the Byzantine Empire.**

Ioan. Stradanus inuent.

Left **A section of an early-sixteenth-century map of China that shows the route taken by the Italian explorer Marco Polo in the late thirteenth century.**

Marc Aurel Stein *c. 1862–1943*

As a young man Marc Aurel Stein was fascinated by Hsüan-tsang's account of his journey to India. In 1900 Stein, by then an archaeologist, traveled to central Asia. In the Takla Makan Desert he found ancient Indian artifacts, confirmation of Hsüan-tsang's reports that the region had been populated by Indians as early as 200 BCE.

In 1907, on his second expedition, Stein explored Dunhuang and found the so-called Cave of the Thousand Buddhas. He found magnificent Buddhist paintings and texts, including the *Diamond Sutra,* the world's oldest surviving book. On his third expedition, in 1915, he returned to Dunhuang and discovered an ancient cemetery where silks had been used as burial wrappings. Stein's explorations of the Silk Road renewed interest in the ancient highway and its archaeological treasures.

friar, who was an ambassador of King Louis IX of France.

The most famous Silk Road traveler was the Italian explorer Marco Polo, who left Venice in 1271 on a journey that took him over the Pamirs (mountains in present-day Tajikistan) and then south of the Takla Makan Desert and across the Gobi Desert to the court of Kublai Khan in 1275. His account of his travels to and around China is regarded as one of the great travel books of all time.

DECLINE

The accession in 1368 of China's Ming dynasty, whose rulers forbade foreigners to enter China, marked the end of the Silk Road as a major international highway. Given also the enmity of the Muslim powers who controlled the Near East, Europeans began to search for alternative routes to East Asia. Their search culminated in the great Portuguese and Spanish ocean voyages of the fifteenth and sixteenth centuries.

SEE ALSO
- Faxian
- Polo, Marco
- Zhang Qian

SMITH, JEDEDIAH STRONG

JEDEDIAH STRONG SMITH (1799–1831) was one of the mountain men, bold and adventurous trappers who pioneered the exploration of the Rocky Mountain region of the United States while hunting for furs. After his discovery in Wyoming of the South Pass, a relatively easy passage across the Rockies, the way was open for wagon trains to follow the Oregon Trail to the Pacific coast. Thus began the settlement of western America.

Below **A deeply religious man, Jedediah Smith indulged in few of the vices for which mountain men were notorious.**

EARLY LIFE

Jedediah Strong Smith was born in central New York, where he lived for about twelve years. Around 1811 the family moved to a Pennsylvania town on Lake Erie. Smith began to work on a Lake Erie boat when he was thirteen. A few years later, he left home and moved farther west. By 1822 he had reached Saint Louis.

JOINING WILLIAM ASHLEY

Shortly after arriving in Saint Louis, Smith was hired as a hunter for William Henry Ashley's new fur business. Smith set out for the Rocky Mountains in May 1822 and spent the summer and winter hunting and trapping in the mountains near the upper Missouri River. In 1823 he was named to lead an expedition to the Black Hills of South Dakota. On that trip he was surprised by a grizzly bear, which tore away the top of his head from his left eye to his right ear. A companion stitched Smith's scalp back together, and after resting for ten days, he was ready to move again.

Through the rest of 1823 and early 1824, Smith and his crew trapped in the northern Rockies. It was during these travels that Smith found the South Pass. Though the pass had been used twelve years earlier by a party of John Jacob Astor's fur traders, details of the route had not been widely distributed. Smith, on the other hand, let others know about the pass at every opportunity.

Later that year, Smith met a party of fur traders from the British-owned Hudson's Bay Company. Traveling with them for a while, he gathered useful information about British operations in the northern Rockies.

The Settlement of Oregon

Jedediah Strong Smith played a significant role in the westward expansion of the United States. On his return to Saint Louis after finding the South Pass, Smith wrote to the American secretary of war. He explained that the South Pass could easily be used by wagons and praised the fertile land of the Willamette River valley, in western Oregon. He also pointed out that the extensive fur trapping carried out by the British in Oregon violated an agreement made in 1818 with the United States. The letter helped to spur American interest in Oregon. Within a few years, thousands of settlers traveled the Oregon Trail, from Missouri over the South Pass to the Willamette valley. By 1846 the American presence had grown so strong that the British yielded the area to the United States.

Below By 1908, when these Arizona trappers were photographed, the trapping business was much less widespread than it had been in the 1820s.

1799
Jedediah Strong Smith is born in New York.

1811
Begins working on Lake Erie.

1822
Joins the company run by William Henry Ashley and Andrew Henry.

1823
Is caught in a Native American attack on Ashley's men and is later mauled by a bear.

1824
Crosses over the South Pass.

1826–1827
Crosses southwest into California and returns to the Great Salt Lake via the Great Basin.

1827–1829
Travels to California and Oregon.

1830
Sells his interest in the fur company and buys a farm in Missouri.

1831
Is killed on an expedition to Santa Fe.

Above **Smith's crossing of the Great Salt Desert—a remarkable feat of endurance and willpower—was captured in this painting by Frederic Remington.**

TREKKING THE FAR WEST

In 1825 Smith took part in the first trappers' rendezvous, an annual gathering at which trappers exchanged the furs they had collected for fresh supplies. The following year he and two other mountain men bought Ashley's company.

Later in 1826 Smith set out on an epic journey. He led a small party southwest from the Great Salt Lake to the Colorado River. From there they moved west across the difficult Mojave Desert and reached southern California, then in Mexican hands. They continued north up the San Joaquin valley as far as the American River. Although they were unable to cross the high, snowy Sierra Nevadas of eastern California in February 1827, they succeeded three months later, by which time the party had been reduced to Smith and two others.

Smith and his companions then had to cross the scorching desert of the Great Basin,

the plateau that lies between the Rocky Mountains and the Sierra Nevadas. Their journey was difficult, and they were often without food or water. On one occasion they buried themselves up to the neck in a slightly shaded hill of sand in order to cool down. The men finally reached the rendezvous, east of the Great Salt Lake, in July. Smith and his fellow travelers had been away for nearly a year and had been given up for dead. "My arrival," Smith wrote, "caused a considerable bustle in camp."

About a month later, Smith set out again along the same southern route to California. On this expedition the Mojave people attacked his small troop and killed ten of the nineteen men. In Oregon the party was attacked again, and this time only Smith and two others survived. With the help of agents from the Hudson's Bay Company, they recovered the furs taken by the Native Americans who had attacked them and eventually headed east. They joined the trappers' rendezvous of 1829 in eastern Idaho.

A Trapper's End

In 1830 Smith decided to give up the hard life of a mountain man. He and his partners sold their company to four colleagues, including Jim Bridger, and Smith went back to Missouri. In spring of the following year, Smith and some companions left Missouri on a trading trip to Santa Fe, New Mexico. One day in May, about halfway to his destination, Smith went ahead of the rest of the party to look for water. He was attacked by a small party of Comanches and killed.

In an 1827 letter sent back to Saint Louis, Smith described the Great Salt Desert, which he had just crossed:

The country between the mountain[s] and this lake [Great Salt Lake] is completely barren, and entirely destitute of game. We frequently traveled two days, without water, over sandy deserts, where no sign of vegetation was to be seen. In some of the rocky hills we found water, and occasionally small bands of Indians, who . . . subsisted upon grass seeds, grass-hoppers, (etc.). On arriving at the Great Salt Lake, we had but one horse and one mule remaining, and they so poor, they could scarcely carry the little camp [equipment] we had with us. The balance of the horses we were compelled to eat as they gave out.

Letter to William Clark, July 12, 1827

Jedediah Strong Smith (1826–1829)

Left **With his trailblazing journeys in the American West, which included the first west-to-east crossing of the Sierra Nevadas and the Great Basin, Jedediah Strong Smith contributed greatly to the opening up of the area for settlement.**

SEE ALSO

- Ashley, William Henry
- Astor, John Jacob
- Bridger, Jim
- Carson, Kit

SMITH, JOHN

THE ENGLISH SOLDIER AND EXPLORER John Smith (1580–1631) became the leader of Jamestown, Virginia, the first permanent English settlement in North America. In later life he was a successful author and an enthusiastic supporter of the colonization of America. He is remembered by many as the man who was captured by a group of American Indians and subsequently rescued by the chief's daughter, Pocahontas.

Below **This portrait of Captain John Smith, first governor of Virginia, was painted around 1616.**

EARLY LIFE

John Smith was born in Willoughby, in Lincolnshire, central England. The son of a farmer, Smith attended a local school and was apprenticed to a merchant at the age of fifteen. A year later he traveled to the Netherlands and joined Dutch forces fighting for independence from Spain. Smith gained a reputation as a brave and fearless soldier, and in 1602 he joined a Hungarian army fighting against the Turks. Having been captured by Turks, he was sold into slavery in Russia but managed to escape by murdering his slave master. During the next few years he traveled throughout Europe and visited north Africa.

PROMISE OF A NEW WORLD

In 1606 Smith returned to England. An adventurer by nature, it was perhaps inevitable that he turned his attention to the Americas, the New World opening up across the Atlantic that held promise of uncharted land and untapped riches. In 1585 an expedition funded by Sir Walter Raleigh had attempted

1580
John Smith is born in Willoughby, central England.

1595
Is apprenticed to a merchant.

1596
Joins the Dutch army fighting the Spanish.

1602
While fighting the Turks in Hungary, is captured and enslaved in Russia.

1602–1605
Escapes from Russia and travels throughout Europe and North Africa.

DECEMBER 19, 1606
Sets sail for Virginia with a party of 105 colonists selected by the Virginia Company.

1607
Jamestown is established; Smith is appointed to the governing council. Later, is captured by Chief Powhatan and saved by Pocahontas.

Pocahontas *c. 1595–1617*

Born near Jamestown, Virginia, Pocahontas, whose given name was Matoaka, was Chief Powhatan's favorite daughter. Powhatan captured John Smith while Smith was on a trading mission along the Chickahominy River in Virginia. Smith claimed that the young girl had prevented his execution by taking his head in her arms and laying her own head on top to save him from being bludgeoned to death. In the following years Pocahontas tried to bring peace between the settlers and the Native Americans. She eventually moved to Jamestown, converted to Christianity, and at her baptism took the name Rebecca. In 1616 she married an English settler named John Rolfe and traveled with him to England. She died of smallpox on the voyage back to Virginia in 1617.

Above **The story of Pocahontas saving the life of John Smith has inspired a number of artworks, such as this nineteenth-century American painting.**

1608
Is elected president of Jamestown.

1609
Is injured and returns to England.

1612
Smith's map of the Chesapeake Bay region is published in Oxford, England.

1614
Smith maps areas of New England.

JUNE 21, 1631
Dies and is buried at Saint Sepulchre's Church in London.

to colonize Virginia (named in honor of Elizabeth I, who was called the Virgin Queen), but the settlements had failed to thrive and were eventually abandoned. Nevertheless, the area remained a tempting proposition, and in 1606 the Virginia Company was granted permission to colonize Virginia in the name of King James I. After investing money in the company, on December 19 Smith himself set sail across the Atlantic.

VOYAGE TO VIRGINIA

The voyage to Virginia took four months. Of the 105 colonists on board the three small ships, most were members of the gentry. Many of them did not like Smith, whose headstrong and confident manner was deemed unacceptable in one from the lower classes. Tension grew on the journey, and at one point Smith was accused of mutiny.

In April 1607 the colonists landed at Chesapeake Bay, off Cape Henry (named after James I's son). Having decided upon the location for their new settlement, they named it Jamestown, in honor of the king.

LIFE IN JAMESTOWN

Life in the colony proved difficult. The area was swampy, and there was little freshwater. Disease, particularly typhoid, spread quickly, and many colonists died. Few settlers were laborers, and many of the gentry struggled with the hard work needed to establish the settlement. The first harvest failed, and the colonists faced starvation. The native people, an Algonquian nation, terrorized the settlers and stole their supplies.

The rough, tough Smith took the role of leader of the struggling community. His leadership was especially important during the dreadful winter of 1607–1608, when the settlement looked doomed to fail. He organized the workforce and took tremendous risks by heading into Native American territory to bargain for food.

In 1608 Smith explored the Chesapeake Bay area. He mapped parts of the lower

Right **John Smith's extensive surveys of the Chesapeake Bay region revealed much about the area but dashed hopes of an easy passage to the Pacific.**

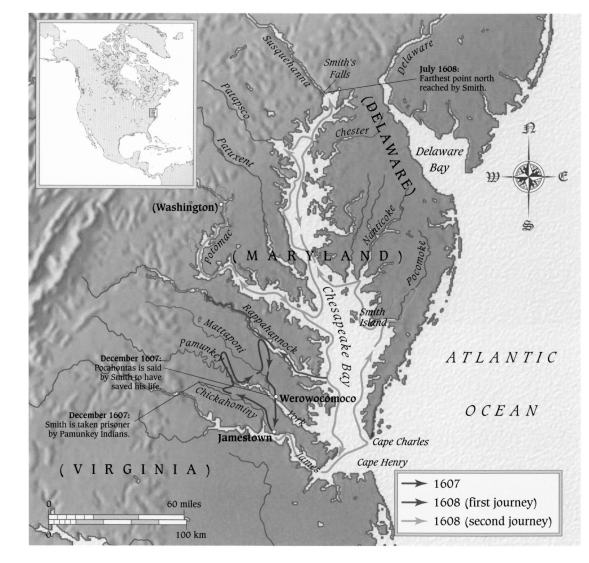

Left **In their vivd depiction of the natural abundance of New England, Smith's maps of Virginia, such as this one from 1612, were an important part of his campaign to promote English overseas colonization.**

course of the Potomac River as far north as present-day Georgetown, a part of Washington, DC. On his return to Jamestown, he was elected president.

RETURN TO ENGLAND

In 1609 Smith was badly injured in a gunpowder explosion. He returned to England, where he campaigned to promote the colonization of America. He visited America again in 1614 to explore the coastline of New England (a name he himself chose for the area) and wrote about his experiences when he returned to England. His published works include *A Description of New England* (1616) and *The Generall Historie of Virginia, New England and the Summer Isles* (1624). Although some of his accounts are considered unreliable—he is suspected of exaggerating his own achievements—he gave his readers a taste of the New World. He also gave them an insight into the appalling conditions that the settlers had endured in their first winter at Jamestown.

In 1624 John Smith described with grim irony the extreme hunger the settlers faced in Jamestown:

Nay, so great was our famine, that a Salvage [savage] we slew, and buried, the poorer sort tooke him up againe and eat him, and so did divers one another boyled and stewed with roots and herbs: And one amongst the rest did kill his wife, powdered her, and had eaten part of her before it was knowne, for which hee was executed, as hee well deserved; now whether shee was better roasted, boyled or carbonado'd, I know not, but of such a dish as powdered wife I never heard of.

The Generall Historie of Virginia, New England and the Summer Isles

Smith neither married nor had children before he died in London, in 1631. He is regarded by many in the United States as a hero, and in 1909 a statue of him was erected in Jamestown.

SEE ALSO

• Great Britain

• Raleigh, Walter

SMITHSONIAN INSTITUTION

ESTABLISHED IN WASHINGTON, DC, IN 1846, the Smithsonian Institution quickly became a museum and research center of national importance. Since its early days, the institution has received records and artifacts collected by explorers and has sponsored numerous expeditions of its own. Now one of the world's most important scientific institutions, the Smithsonian continues to fund exploratory research and to display collections that shed light on the mysteries of the earth and space.

Above **The first Smithsonian building, designed by James Renwick Jr. in a combination of early Gothic and Romanesque styles, was largely destroyed in a disastrous fire in 1865.**

DECIDING THE FATE OF A FORTUNE

James Lewis Smithson (1765–1829), also known as James Macie, was an English scientist who devoted himself to research in chemistry, geology, and mineralogy. In 1832 the mineral Smithsonite was named in his honor. Smithson left his large inherited fortune to his nephew Henry Hungerford, but his will included the instruction that, if Hungerford should die without heirs, the money was to be used "to found at Washington, under the name of the Smithsonian Institution, an Establishment for the increase and diffusion of knowledge." Smithson's reasons for leaving his fortune to the United States are unclear. He never visited the country and had few contacts with Americans. Whatever his motives, his unusual bequest came into effect in 1835, when Hungerford died childless.

In July 1838 Richard Rush, the lawyer handling the bequest, set sail for New York with eleven boxes containing almost 105,000 gold sovereigns, as well as Smithson's library and

Joseph Henry *1797–1878*

*I*n Joseph Henry the Smithsonian Institution was fortunate to have a man of great energy and vision as its first secretary. Henry, secretary from 1846 to 1878, believed that the Smithsonian should play an active part in increasing the sum of scientific knowledge. He set up a network of volunteers who took daily weather readings around the United States and sent the data to Washington by telegraph. Soon North America's first daily weather charts were being produced.

The journal *Smithsonian Contributions to Knowledge* was first published and distributed free of charge to colleges and scholars in 1848. In 1849, to keep the cost of buying academic books and equipment from Europe as low as possible, Henry helped to set up the International Exchange Service.

scientific collection. The sovereigns were melted down to yield gold worth more than half a million dollars, in those days a vast sum of money.

BIRTH OF AN INSTITUTION

There was great public debate about what should be done with Smithson's fortune. John Quincy Adams, the former president, suggested building a national astronomical observatory, while others suggested a national university, a national library, or a national college to train teachers of science. In 1846 the act establishing the Smithsonian Institution was finally adopted. It provided for a museum of natural history, an art gallery, a scientific laboratory, a library, and public lecture halls. A building to house the new institution opened in 1855. Its first secretary was Joseph Henry, a distinguished scientist who saw the institution's primary role as the promotion of scientific research.

THE SMITHSONIAN GROWS

Henry's assistant secretary, Spencer Fullerton Baird, wanted the Smithsonian to become the premier repository for scientific and historical treasures in the United States. In 1878 Congress made the institution responsible for setting up an American national museum. By 1887 the institution housed more than 2.5 million items. At the beginning of the twenty-first century, the institution had grown to include fourteen major museums in Washington and two in New York. Its archives hold millions of documents, photographs, films, and artifacts of all kinds.

Above **Joseph Henry told his American colleagues that the Smithsonian Institution would "stimulate the talent of our country to original research and pour fresh material on the apex of the pyramid of science and thus enlarge its base."**

between 1838 and 1842. Other U.S. agencies working in little-known territory, such as the army's Pacific Railway surveying teams and the U.S.-Mexican Boundary Commission, deposited their finds with the institution.

Among the early expeditions the institution helped to sponsor were the U.S. Navy *Polaris* expedition to the North Pole under Captain Charles Hall, between 1871 and 1873, and the African expedition, led by the former president Theodore Roosevelt in 1909. Roosevelt's expedition added over 11,400 items to the museum's collections, including over 5,000 animal skins.

PUSHING BACK THE LIMITS

Often working with other leading scientific institutions, teams from the Smithsonian explore the deep oceans and outer space. Marine scientists investigate undersea geology and patterns of biodiversity, evolution, and extinction among marine species. The Smithsonian Astrophysical Observatory collaborates with Harvard College Observatory and the National Aeronautics and Space Administration (NASA) on the Chandra project. Launched into high orbit in 1999, the Chandra X-ray Observatory picks up radiation from high-energy sources, such as exploded stars. Smithsonian researchers were involved in a mission, launched in 2003, to explore the geology of Mars and a mission to Mercury launched in 2004.

A NEW FOCUS FOR EXPLORATION

In the twenty-first century the science of exploration has shifted its focus from the search for new territories to the investigation of aspects of the earth other than its surface

Above **The Smithsonian preserves evidence of Native American cultures that were lost with the westward spread of settlers. This mask was made between 1800 and 1850 by the Haida, who were native to the Queen Charlotte Islands (off British Columbia).**

EXPLORATION AND COLLECTION

Since its earliest days, the Smithsonian Institution has been involved in exploration. In the 1850s Spencer Baird encouraged naturalists, geologists, and U.S. Army officers stationed in the West to collect Indian artifacts, natural specimens, minerals, and fossils for the Smithsonian. Soon the Smithsonian became the natural repository for artifacts gathered on a wide range of exploring expeditions. In 1858 the institution acquired records and specimens from the U.S. Exploring Expedition, which had explored the Pacific Ocean and circumnavigated the globe

The Institution and Alaska

*I*n 1859 Spencer Baird sent Robert Kennicott to explore the Yukon, in northwestern Canada and Alaska (a territory then known as Russian America). Kennicott returned four years later with a vast collection of specimens from the far north of the Americas. The institution sent a second fact-finding scientific expedition to the Yukon in 1865. The work of these two expeditions raised American awareness of the great wealth and importance of Alaska. The information gathered by the Smithsonian expeditions helped to persuade the U.S. government to purchase Alaska from Czar Alexander II of Russia in 1867.

geography. The Smithsonian Institution supports and sponsors modern-day exploration; the Smithsonian Environmental Research Center at Chesapeake Bay, for example, investigates the impact of human activity on the coastal environment. The Center for Earth and Planetary Studies uses remote sensing to analyze patterns of environmental change. The long Smithsonian tradition of enquiry and the advancement of human knowledge continues.

SEE ALSO

• Museums • Remote Sensing
• Space Exploration • Underwater Exploration

Below **The Castle, the only part of the original Smithsonian building to survive the disastrous fire of 1865, was used as a family home by Joseph Henry. It is now the administrative center of the institution, which currently comprises fifteen major museums.**

1829
James Smithson dies.

1846
U.S. Congress sets up the Smithsonian Institution.

1855
Smithsonian's first buildings open.

1859
The Smithsonian sponsors its first expedition, to the Yukon (in Alaska and Canada).

1878
Spencer Baird succeeds Joseph Henry as secretary.

1890
Smithsonian Astrophysical Observatory opens.

1910
National Museum of Natural History opens.

1964
National Museum of American History opens.

1976
National Air and Space Museum opens.

SOLAR SYSTEM

THE SOLAR SYSTEM, the immediate neighborhood of Earth, has the Sun at its center and a number of celestial bodies in perpetual orbit around the Sun or around each other. In all, the solar system comprises the Sun, nine planets, over sixty moons, millions of asteroids, and billions of comets. The planets Mercury, Venus, Mars, Jupiter, and Saturn were identified by ancient astronomers. Uranus, Neptune, and Pluto were discovered between the eighteenth and twentieth centuries.

Below **This picture is a montage of images taken by the *Voyager* spacecraft of the planets and four of Jupiter's moons; in the foreground is Earth's Moon.**

UNDERSTANDING THE SOLAR SYSTEM

In the second century CE, the Greek astronomer Ptolemy developed a geocentric (earth-centered) view of the universe that was based on the work of previous astronomers and on his own observations of the night sky. His theory, that the Sun, Moon, and planets orbited Earth, went largely unchallenged until the sixteenth century, when the Polish astronomer Nicolaus Copernicus posited a heliocentric (sun-centered) universe, with Earth and the other planets orbiting the Sun. Copernicus thought that the planets followed perfectly circular orbits, but in 1605 the German Johannes Kepler demonstrated that planets follow elliptical (oval) paths.

Observing the Sun

The Sun is by far the largest object in the solar system. It consists predominantly of hydrogen and has an inner core of helium. The surface temperature of the Sun is about 9,930° F (5,500° C), while the temperature at its core measures about 60 million° F (15.6 million° C).

Since its launch on December 2, 1995, the Solar and Heliospheric Observatory (SOHO), a space telescope operated jointly by the European Space Agency and NASA, has collected data on solar activity, including sunspots (regions of intense magnetic energy on the surface), solar flares (eruptions of energy from the surface), and prominences (plasma clouds in the solar atmosphere).

In 1687 the English physicist Isaac Newton published his laws of motion, which offered a unified way of describing the movement of all objects, from the tiniest particles to the largest celestial bodies. Newton's theory of gravity gave a satisfactory explanation of the paths followed by orbiting bodies, and astronomers' understanding of the solar system was greatly enhanced by his work.

ORIGINS OF THE SOLAR SYSTEM

Newton's influence lasted into the twentieth century, when the works of Albert Einstein (1879–1955) placed theories of motion into a wider context. Einstein's special and general theories of relativity postulated a mathematical relationship between gravity and electromagnetic energy and gave astronomers an entirely new way of looking at the universe. Increasingly powerful intruments picked up electromagnetic radiation emitting from distant sources, and astronomers began to advance theories about the origin of the solar system and of the universe as a whole.

In 1929 Edwin Hubble, an American astronomer, observed galaxies moving away from Earth. Hubble's findings, which suggested that the universe was expanding, inspired the big bang model of the formation of the universe. According to the big bang theory, around ten billion years ago the universe exploded out of a highly compressed state of high temperature and density.

Most modern astronomers believe that the solar system formed 4.6 billion years ago, when a ball of gas and dust collapsed into a flat, spinning disk. The temperature in the center of the disk became so hot that a star started to burn. As the matter surrounding the star was flung around in concentric circles, it gradually coalesced to form orbiting planets and other celestial bodies.

Above **Fully assembled, checked, and fueled for flight, the Solar and Heliospheric Observatory (SOHO) is ready to be enclosed in the covering that will protect it during launch.**

Sun and the Moon, Venus is often the brightest object in the sky. Known as the morning star or the evening star (since at these times it shines most brightly), Venus was an important reference point for explorers navigating by observation of the sky.

EARTH

Earth is the only planet in the solar system—and indeed the only place in the universe—where life is known to exist. Earth is uniquely conditioned to support life in four significant ways: it has a large supply of water; because of its distance from the Sun, the surface temperature is neither too hot nor too cold; its strong magnetic field and atmosphere protect the planet from harmful solar rays; and the blend of chemicals available in the atmosphere and on the surface—especially carbon, oxygen, hydrogen, and nitrogen—is proportioned in such a way as to support life.

Above **This mosaic image of the planet Mercury was created using several images taken by the** *Mariner 10* **space probe in 1974 and 1975. The surface of Mercury is heavily cratered owing to impacts from meteorites. It also has lines of cliffs that are up to 1.9 miles (3 km) high and 311 miles (500 km) long.**

THE HOT PLANETS

Mercury is the planet closest to the Sun. As a result of its proximity to the Sun and its thin atmosphere, Mercury's surface is subject to daytime temperatures as high as 662° F (350° C). At night, however, Mercury can be as cold as −338° F (−170° C). During observations of Mercury in 1973, the space probe *Mariner 10* found a surface marked by craters, lava plains, and low cliffs. In 2004 NASA launched the *Messenger* (*Mercury* *Surface*, *Space* *Environment*, *Geochemistry* and *Ranging*) probe, which will enter into orbit around the planet in 2009.

Venus, roughly the same size as Earth, is positioned between Earth and Mercury. Thick clouds of sulfuric acid conceal the planet's surface and trap carbon dioxide in the atmosphere, the result being an extreme greenhouse effect. The surface of Venus is even hotter than that of Mercury (temperatures often reach 900° F, or 480° C). After the

THE RED PLANET

Mars is the fourth planet from the sun. Its atmosphere contains a high proportion of carbon dioxide, and the surface is covered with iron oxide, which gives the planet its red coloring. Many scientists believe that, of all the planets in the solar system other than Earth, Mars is the most capable of supporting human life. Images of its rocky surface, particularly those taken by the *Pathfinder* and *Global Surveyor* probes in the late 1990s, have revealed canyons and ravines that may have been formed by flowing water. Although Mars may not have had water on its surface for four billion years, some astronomers hope that water will be found below the surface. In 2004, NASA released two robotic exploration rovers, *Spirit* and *Opportunity*, onto Mars. Their analysis of the planet's surface conditions and atmosphere was conducted with a view to assessing the feasibility of a future manned mission to Earth's closest neighbor.

How Many Moons?

*H*ighly sensitive modern telescopes are detecting the presence of more and more moons throughout the solar system. A moon is defined as any natural satellite orbiting a planet, a definition that encompasses everything from chunks of space rock to Ganymede, a moon of Jupiter that is larger than the planet Neptune. By 2004 sixty-one moons had been discovered orbiting Jupiter, and thirty-one around Saturn. Uranus has twenty-seven moons, and Neptune thirteen. Mars has just two, Earth and Pluto have one each, and Mercury and Venus have no moons. Many of the smaller newly discovered moons are described as irregular moons. They follow large, elliptical orbits and travel around the planet in a direction opposite to that of the planet's rotation (a path known as a retrograde orbit).

Left Laboratory engineers prepare the *Mars Global Surveyor* spacecraft for launch by placing it in a protective canister.

Right **The Great Red Spot on Jupiter's surface, an ancient high-pressure storm, is three times the size of Earth.**

THE GIANT PLANETS

Jupiter and Saturn are the largest planets in the solar system. Both have a small, solid core surrounded by a thick gaseous atmosphere. The atmosphere of both planets contains gases that do not mix. High winds blow these gases into differently colored stripes. Jupiter, the fifth planet from the Sun, is also the largest. Perhaps its most prominent feature is the Great Red Spot. First observed by the French astronomer Dian Domenico Cassini in 1665, the Great Red Spot is a whirling eddy of gases that looks much like a permanently raging storm. Saturn is the sixth planet from the Sun. Its prominent ring system is among the most spectacular phenomena in the solar system. The rings, which consist of particles of rock, dust, and ice, have a diameter of 168,000 miles (270,000 km) but are never more than 0.06 miles (100 m) thick.

THE FAR PLANETS

The planets farthest from the Sun, Uranus, Neptune, and Pluto, are all relatively recent

c. 160 CE
Ptolemy's *Almagest* describes a universe with Earth at its center, orbited by the Sun, the Moon, and five planets (Mercury, Venus, Mars, Jupiter, and Saturn).

1543
Nicolaus Copernicus puts forward the theory that Earth revolves around the Sun.

1610
Galileo Galilei discovers four moons of Jupiter (Callisto, Europa, Io, and Ganymede).

1781
William Herschel discovers Uranus.

1846
The work of a number of astronomers leads to the discovery of Neptune.

1930
The American astronomer Clyde W. Tombaugh identifies Pluto.

discoveries. Uranus is the only planet in the solar system to spin on its side. It has a solid core and an atmosphere of gas and ice. Neptune has a solid core, a layer of ice, and a thick atmosphere. Pluto, the smallest planet and the farthest from the Sun, has a solid icy surface and very little atmosphere. Since no probes have yet visited Pluto, little is known for certain about this remote planet.

OTHER CELESTIAL BODIES

The asteroid belt consists of thousands of small rocky bodies that orbit the Sun along a path between the orbits of Mars and Jupiter. Comets are similar to asteroids, except that they are made of more volatile material and follow an eccentric orbit that takes them far from the Sun for long periods and close to the Sun for short periods. When they approach the Sun, comets shine more brightly, and many trail a tail of dust.

A meteoroid is a particle of rock falling through space. When a meteoroid enters Earth's atmosphere, it burns up and creates a streak of light that is commonly called a shooting, or falling, star. A meteoroid that survives its journey to Earth intact is known as a meteorite.

Below **The French mathematician Urbain-Jean-Joseph Leverrier correctly predicted the existence and position of the planet Neptune in the 1840s.**

SEE ALSO
- Astronomical Instruments • Astronomy • Satellites • SETI
- Space Exploration

Soto, Hernando de

FEW EARLY SPANISH EXPLORERS of the Americas had a more richly varied and interesting life than Hernando de Soto (c. 1497–1542). After making his fortune trading in the Caribbean, de Soto played a key role in the Spanish defeat of the Incan Empire in South America. Several years later, lured by rumors of vast riches, he led the first major European expedition into the interior of North America.

CONQUEST OF THE INCAS

Hernando de Soto's adventures in the New World, the newly discovered territories of the Americas, began when he sailed to the Caribbean in 1514. He gained a reputation as an able leader and soon made a fortune, largely from trading in slaves. In 1530 he lent two ships to Francisco Pizarro, who wanted to investigate reports of vast wealth that was rumored to exist in South America. Two years later de Soto became second in command and captain of horse (chief cavalry officer) in Pizarro's expedition to conquer the kingdom of the Incas, a powerful empire centered on present-day Peru.

De Soto discovered the Inca Road, the great highway that ran through the Andes Mountains and led to the Incan capital, Cuzco. He also played a key role in the defeat of the Incas at the battle of Cajamarca. He was the first Spaniard to meet with the Incan king, Atahualpa, with whom he was on relatively amicable terms. When Pizarro ordered Atahualpa's execution, de Soto was probably genuinely shocked. He returned to Spain in 1536 with one of the largest fortunes ever taken from the New World. He even lent money to the Spanish king, Charles I, an act that won him great political influence.

EXPLORATION OF NORTH AMERICA

In April 1538 de Soto sold all his property to fund a new adventure: a conquest of Florida and the surrounding territory. He had heard rumors that the region boasted even more gold and silver than Peru. Having been declared governor of Cuba and lord of Florida by Charles I, de Soto planned a journey to take up his governorship. He set sail for the North American mainland on May 18, 1539, with a party that comprised around six hundred soldiers and several hundred servants, camp followers, and Indian slaves.

Below **Hernando de Soto was one of the most important figures in the early European exploration of the United States.**

Francisco Pizarro c. 1475–1541

_F_rancisco Pizarro first set sail from Spain for the Americas in 1509 and went on to lead several expeditions along the western coast of South America. In 1529 King Charles I of Spain granted him the governorship of a vast unexplored area of what is now Peru. After landing near the mouth of the Santiago River, Pizarro's expedition reached the Incan city of Cajamarca in 1532. At Cajamarca the Spaniards massacred many of the native people and captured and imprisoned the Incan king, Atahualpa. Although a vast ransom in gold was handed over to secure Atahualpa's release, Pizarro nevertheless had him executed. Pizarro later seized the Incan capital, Cuzco, and established his own capital, Lima, in 1535. In 1541 Pizarro was assassinated at Lima by supporters of a rival conquistador.

Left **A contemporary portrait of Francisco Pizarro, the often ruthless Spanish conqueror of Peru.**

c. 1497
Hernando de Soto is born in Badajoz, southwestern Spain.

1514
Sails with Pedro Arias Dávila's expedition to the Caribbean.

1515–1527
Makes his fortune in the Caribbean and Nicaragua.

1532
Takes part, with Francisco Pizarro, in the conquest of the Incas.

1536
Returns to Spain.

1539
Lands in Florida.

1540
Fights a fierce battle against Native Americans at Mauvila.

1541
Sights Mississippi River.

1542
Dies near the Mississippi River.

Having spent the winter in Florida, in 1540 de Soto and his men traveled north through present-day Georgia and then northwest via the Carolinas to Tennessee before heading back south to link up with supply ships.

The expedition faced two serious obstacles. The first, entirely of the men's own making, was a tendency to be lured deeper into the interior of the North American continent by the promise of pearls, gold, and silver. Rumors of such wealth were often started by Native Americans, who wanted the invaders to move on and leave them in peace. The second major obstacle, the general hostility of native people, was to a certain extent inherited by de Soto. Members of the previous Spanish expedition to southern North America, led by Pánfilo de Narváez, had treated the Native Americans with violence and cruelty. Native Americans who had met or heard of Narváez guarded themselves against similar treatment by de Soto by attacking and harrying him from the outset.

After discovering that some of his dispirited men were preparing to desert and seize the supply ships before he reached them, de Soto changed his route and headed west. He decided to try to reach New Spain (present-day Mexico) by land, reasoning that the men would be less likely to desert when they were so far from the supply ships. He crossed the Mississippi River in the summer of 1541 and spent the winter in northwestern Arkansas. The following spring he headed back toward the Mississippi, where he fell ill with fever. He died in May 1542, and his body was committed to the waters of the mighty river.

Luis de Moscoso Alvarado (1505–1551), de Soto's old friend and second in command, was the obvious choice to take over after the death of de Soto. Although his actions had led to the loss of most of the expedition's horses in March 1541, his position was accepted, and his decision to head home was popular. He led a fruitless trek southwest into Texas and back into Arkansas. He then supervised the

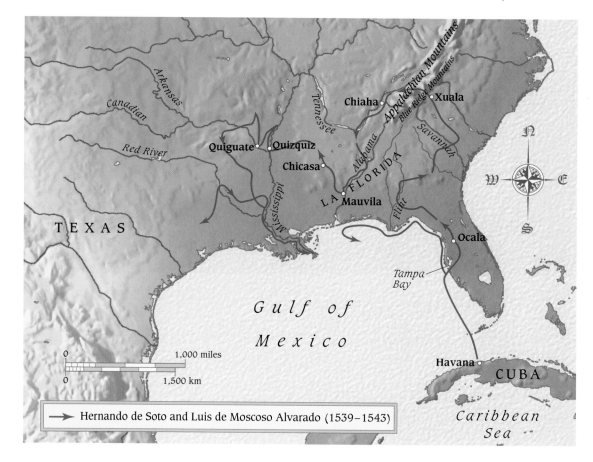

Right **De Soto's somewhat errant journey through the present-day southeastern United States afforded significant glimpses of the geography of the newly discovered continent, particularly of the Savannah, Mississippi, and Arkansas Rivers.**

Hernando de Soto and Luis de Moscoso Alvarado (1539–1543)

The Battle of Mauvila

*T*he settlement of Mauvila, near the modern town of Mobile, Alabama, was the scene of one of the bloodiest early battles fought between American Indians and the European invaders. Hernando de Soto and his men fought their way into Mauvila in early October 1540. They killed between 2,500 and 3,000 enemy warriors and burned the settlement. De Soto's own losses were considerably less—around 25 men were killed and 150 wounded, including de Soto himself. Nevertheless, the loss of many of his horses and much of his equipment severely weakened the expedition.

building of seven ships, in which the 322 survivors floated down the Mississippi. Having become, in the process, the first Europeans to travel down that river, they finally reached New Spain in September 1543.

LEGACY

De Soto had crossed the entire southeastern corner of North America. Accounts of his expedition, written by his secretary and a Portuguese man known only as a "gentleman of Elvas," revealed the region's principal characteristics. In 1584 Jeronimo de Chaves, the Spanish royal mapmaker, compiled a map that was probably based on the account of the gentleman of Elvas. It was the first printed map to show the lower course of the Mississippi River and the Appalachian Mountains. Hernando de Soto had led the first European exploration of the southeastern United States. Less happily, de Soto's expedition worsened relations between Europeans and Native Americans, an unfortunate legacy that would endure for centuries.

SEE ALSO

- Narváez, Pánfilo de • Núñez de Balboa, Vasco
- Ponce de León, Juan • Spain

Above **This nineteenth-century engraving captures some of the tumult and excitement that must have accompanied de Soto's landing in Florida.**

SOUTHERN CONTINENT

LONG AFTER THE WORLD'S lands and seas had been mapped in rough outline, the southernmost oceans remained a complete mystery. Explorers from the sixteenth to the eighteenth centuries searched with great zeal for the vast and populous southern continent first proposed by ancient philosophers. As voyage after voyage penetrated farther into perilous (but empty) southern waters, the extent of any possible southern continent began to recede—and with it hopes for one last major discovery.

TERRA INCOGNITA

Around 550 BCE the Greek astronomer Anaximander of Miletus proposed a circular world. Soon after, the philosopher Pythagoras suggested that the world was spherical. In the fourth century BCE Aristotle, one of the most important of all ancient Greek philosophers, reasoned that, since the world was by nature symmetrical, there must be a cold zone in the south to balance the frozen lands that were known to exist in the north. Aristotle and his followers proposed five climate zones; a cold north, a temperate band, a hot equatorial zone, another temperate band, and a cold southern zone. In the second century CE the influential Greek geographer Ptolemy incorporated the work of the ancient philosophers in his world map, which included *Terra Incognita* ("unknown land"), a huge continent whose northern boundary was at 20° south latitude.

THE SEARCH BEGINS

Ptolemy's *Geographica* was rediscovered in the fifteenth century. By 1480 printed versions of Ptolemy's maps were widely available, and so the accepted picture of the world at the dawn of the Age of Discovery included a southern continent.

The Portuguese pressed down the coast of Africa and found the continent's southern point in 1497, when Vasco da Gama rounded

Herman Moll (1654–1732), one of the most popular cartographers of his day, believed in a vast southern continent:

The southern unknown region, or Terra australis incognita, is a vast tract of land as we judge by the coasts. I have distinguished the parts of it by the several names given it by Pilots and Captains who have sailed by them. . . . The inhabitants are white, of a large stature, strong, industrious and courageous.

Quoted in J. N. L. Baker, *Mythical Lands in History*

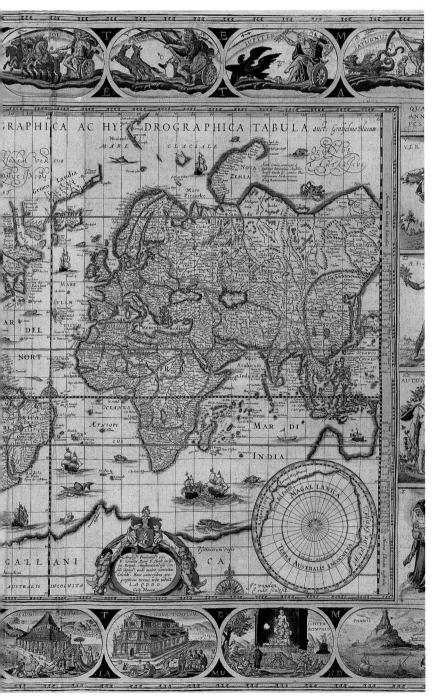

the Cape of Good Hope. Da Gama's journey proved that no southern continent was joined to Africa. On the other side of the Atlantic, the Spanish pressed down the coast of South America and found a passage to the Pacific Ocean. When Ferdinand Magellan passed through the Strait of Magellan in 1520, many geographers speculated that the land he sighted to the south of the strait might be the northern tip of a southern continent.

In 1578 the English sailor Francis Drake followed Magellan's route through the Strait of Magellan but was blown back by storms as he entered the Pacific. Thus, it was by chance that he saw that the land to the south of the strait (Tierra del Fuego) was in fact merely an island.

THE SOUTH PACIFIC

Magellan's voyage across the Pacific revealed the vast extent of that ocean. Many explorers assumed that some landmass must fill its southern portion. Spanish explorers in Peru heard Incan myths of rich lands to the west. From 1605 to 1606, Pedro Fernández de Quirós, fired by dreams of being a new Columbus, led a voyage west and found the island now named Vanuatu. Convinced that it was the longed-for continent, he named it La Austrialia del Espíritu Santo.

At the same time, the Dutch were exploring the Pacific from their stronghold in the East Indies. In 1642 Abel Tasman was sent to find out if Australia (then known as New Holland) was part of a southern continent. By making the first European discovery of Tasmania and New Zealand, Tasman demonstrated that the southern continent could not extend as far north as had been supposed.

Left **On this world map by Jan Blaeu (1598–1673), a member of an important Dutch mapmaking dynasty, a vast southern continent fills almost the entire unknown southern portion of the world.**

Above **This eighteenth-century watercolor by John Webber depicts Christmas Harbor in Kerguelen's Land, a barren sub-Antarctic archipelago also known as the Desolation Islands.**

DESOLATION

Over the next hundred years several voyages probed the stormy southern oceans but located only scattered islands. In 1675 Antoine de la Roche discovered South Georgia, around 55° south latitude. In 1700 Edmond Halley sighted icebergs (which always originate on land) at 52°24' S. In 1739 Jean-Baptiste Charles Bouvet de Lozier reached land around 54° S (present-day Bouvet Island). In 1772 Yves-Joseph de Kerguélen-Trémarec boasted that, in the southern Indian Ocean, he had found a temperate populated paradise, which he named New South France. When he returned in 1773 for a closer look, he found only a land of freezing mist and bare rock. (The present-day Kerguelen Islands are also aptly called the Desolation Islands.)

JAMES COOK

On January 17, 1773, sailing south from Africa on his second attempt to find the southern continent, James Cook made the first crossing of the Antarctic Circle. Over the following months he skirted the ice pack eastward and found that there was no large landmass north of 60° S between the longitudes of London

c. 130 CE	1520	1606	1642	1772
The Greek geographer Ptolemy proposes a huge southern continent.	Ferdinand Magellan sights land to the south as he travels from the Atlantic Ocean into the Pacific.	Pedro Fernández de Quirós lands on present-day Vanuatu and believes that he has found the southern continent.	Abel Tasman sails across the southwestern Pacific and discovers Tasmania and New Zealand but no southern continent.	Yves-Joseph de Kerguélen-Trémarec declares (falsely) that he has found a populated southern continent.

and New Zealand. In 1774 and 1775 Cook searched for the southern continent between New Zealand and South America. In the process he sighted South Georgia and the South Sandwich Islands in the South Atlantic and completed a circumnavigation of the world at high southern latitudes. By doing so, Cook finally proved that the southern continent was a myth.

HUNTERS

Cook's records made mention of abundant seals and whales, and hunters seeking profits from fur and oil made for southern waters. In their scramble for new hunting grounds, sealers and whalers discovered many outlying sub-Antarctic islands, including Macquarie Island, the South Shetland Islands, and the South Orkney Islands, discovered respectively by the Australian Frederick Hasselborough (1810), the Englishman William Smith (1819), and the American Nathaniel Palmer (1821).

SIGHTING ANTARCTICA

The question of who first sighted the Antarctic mainland is unresolved. In January 1820 the British naval officer Edward Bransfield sighted distant mountains that may have been on the Antarctic Peninsula. The Russian Fabian Gottlieb von Bellingshausen got to within twenty miles of the Antarctic mainland on January 20, 1820. A competing claim is also made for Nathaniel Palmer. What is certain is that by 1820, the history of Antarctica was beginning—and that of a southern continent was over.

Alexander Dalrymple c. 1737–1808

While conducting research in Madras, India, the Scottish geographer Alexander Dalrymple became convinced of the existence of a vast, populous southern continent, which he named Great South Land. The Royal Society of London recommended Dalrymple to command a voyage to the Pacific, but the Admiralty appointed James Cook. When Cook returned from his second voyage with proof that no such continent existed, Dalrymple attacked him in print.

Above **Alexander Dalrymple (1737–1808) believed passionately in a vast populated southern continent.**

1772–1775
James Cook circumnavigates Antarctica and finally disproves the theory that a great southern continent exists in temperate latitudes.

1820
Fabian Gottlieb von Bellingshausen, Edward Bransfield, and Nathaniel Palmer make sightings of the Antarctic mainland.

SEE ALSO
- Bellingshausen, Fabian Gottlieb von
- Cook, James • Drake, Francis
- Magellan, Ferdinand • Polar Exploration
- Ptolemy • Quirós, Pedro Fernández de
- Tasman, Abel

SPACECRAFT

WITH THE DEVELOPMENT of rocket-fuel-propulsion systems in the early twentieth century, the notion that a vehicle might make a controlled flight into space became a serious consideration. Since the 1957 launch of *Sputnik 1,* the first spacecraft, numerous manned and unmanned spacecraft have journeyed into space. They have fulfilled—and continue to fulfil—a range of purposes, particularly those related to monitoring the earth and exploring space.

Left **Konstantin Tsiolkovsky, a self-educated Russian chemist and physicist, is recognized as a pioneer of space travel.**

ROCKET POWER

In 1891 Hermann Ganswindt, a German inventor, suggested a rocket would generate enough thrust to propel a vehicle beyond the earth's atmosphere. In 1903 Konstantin Tsiolkovsky, a Russian aeronautics expert, published *The Investigation of Space with Reactive Devices,* a theoretical study of rocket-propulsion systems. The American physicist Robert Goddard (1882–1945) designed and tested the first successful liquid-fuel propulsion system, a technology that would be used for manned space flights during the 1960s. In Germany the work of Hermann Oberth (1894–1989) inspired a generation of rocket engineers, including Wernher von Braun (1912–1977), who was in charge of developing Germany's V-2 rocket weapon.

After World War II, rockets were used to launch instruments into the upper atmosphere and near-earth space for scientific research. On October 4, 1957, the Soviet Union launched *Sputnik 1*—the very first satellite to orbit the earth. Since the launch of *Sputnik 1,* thousands of satellites have been launched into earth orbit with a range of purposes, including communications, remote sensing, and navigation.

Gravity Assists

When a spacecraft passes close to a planet, it is subject to that planet's gravitational pull. With subtle manipulations of the spacecraft's direction, it may, as it were, steal some of the planet's orbital momentum and thus increase its velocity with less fuel consumption. The first spacecraft to use a so-called gravity assist was *Mariner 10*. In 1974 that probe used the gravitational pull of the planet Venus to speed it on its way to Mercury. A more sophisticated version of the gravity assist was used on the Galileo mission to Jupiter (launched in 1989) and also on the Cassini mission to Saturn (launched in 1997). No rocket was big enough to launch a spacecraft the size of *Cassini* on a direct course for Saturn, so *Cassini* used gravity assists from two flybys of Venus and one of Earth to boost it into the outer solar system. A final gravity assist from Jupiter enabled it to reach Saturn, where it entered orbit on July 1, 2004.

UNMANNED SPACE PROBES

The first spacecraft to reach the moon was the Soviet Union's *Luna 2*, which did so in 1959. Spherical in shape, with protruding antennae and instruments, *Luna 2* weighed approximately 858 pounds (390 kg). Launched by a modified SS-6 rocket, the spacecraft itself had no propulsion system.

Modern-day spacecraft are equipped with solar panels, which supply energy to batteries. These in turn power the communications equipment. Booster rockets make small adjustments to the spacecraft's course. Gravity-assisted trajectories allow large space probes to travel farther into outer space.

In the early days of space flight, the only way to achieve an extraterrestrial landing of a spacecraft was to allow it to crash into the surface. By the time of the Viking missions to Mars (1975–1976), a soft landing was ensured by a variety of techniques, including parachutes, which slowed the rate of descent, and retro-rockets, which were fired to keep the lander upright as it touched down. Modern spacecraft use airbags to cushion their landing.

Right **At 9:01 AM (EST) on November 16, 1973, the Saturn IB rocket, carrying four astronauts on the third and final mission to the orbiting *Skylab* space station, was launched.**

Left **The *Apollo 15* command module *Kitty Hawk* nears a safe splashdown in the mid-Pacific Ocean.**

American Mercury and Gemini programs laid the ground for the first flights to the moon.

MISSIONS TO THE MOON

The Apollo spacecraft that took astronauts to the moon consisted of three sections: the command module (where the crew lived and worked), the service module (which contained the engine and life-support systems), and the lunar module (which carried two of the crew down to the moon's surface). Giant Saturn V rockets—the largest ever used by NASA—were used to send the spacecraft skyward. Between 1969 and 1972 six Apollo missions achieved successful moon landings.

THE SPACE SHUTTLE

The fact that each spacecraft could be used only once made manned space exploration almost prohibitively expensive. On April 12, 1981, NASA launched the space shuttle, the first partially reusable spacecraft. The shuttle *Columbia* took off from the Kennedy Space Center in Florida and, after a two-day mission, glided down, unpowered, onto the runway at Edwards Airbase in California.

At launch the main engines of the space shuttle ignite, along with two solid-fuel rocket boosters. Two minutes into the flight, the boosters drop away automatically. After

THE FIRST MANNED SPACE FLIGHTS

Developed by the Soviet Union, a Vostok spacecraft was the first to carry a human being into space (Yury Gagarin made a single orbit of the earth aboard *Vostok 1* on April 12, 1961). The Soviet Vostok program and the

---

OCTOBER 4, 1957
Sputnik 1, the first satellite to orbit the earth, is launched by the Soviet Union.

SEPTEMBER 12, 1959
Luna 2, the first spacecraft to reach the moon, is launched.

APRIL 12, 1961
Yury Gagarin orbits the earth in *Vostok 1.*

JULY 20, 1969
Neil Armstrong and Buzz Aldrin step on the moon from *Apollo 11's* landing module, *Eagle.*

APRIL 19, 1971
Salyut 1, the first space station, is launched by the Soviet Union.

MAY 14, 1973
Skylab, the first U.S. space station, is launched.

APRIL 12, 1981
The first space shuttle, *Columbia,* lifts off.

NOVEMBER 15, 1988
Buran, the unmanned Soviet space shuttle, makes its first and only flight into orbit.

OCTOBER 15, 1997
Cassini is launched toward Saturn.

NOVEMBER 20, 1998
The first module of the International Space Station is launched.

FEBRUARY 1, 2003
Following the loss of *Columbia,* space shuttle missions are suspended.

U.S. Space Shuttle Disasters

*T*ragic accidents have destroyed two of the five space shuttles. On January 28, 1986, *Challenger* exploded shortly after takeoff on what would have been its tenth mission. All seven crew members died. An investigation revealed that a faulty seal in a solid rocket booster, combined with unusually cold weather, had triggered the disaster. When *Columbia* was lost during reentry on February 1, 2003, all seven astronauts on board perished. Investigators discovered that a piece of insulating foam had broken loose during the launch and damaged some of the tiles protecting the craft from the intense heat generated during reentry into Earth's atmosphere.

returning to Earth by parachute, they are recovered from the ocean and can be reused on later flights. The external fuel tank, which drops away just before the shuttle goes into orbit, is burned up in the atmosphere.

Five space shuttles have entered service since 1981. They have played a vital role in launching and maintaining satellites and in ferrying crews and materials to the International Space Station. The space shuttle program was suspended in 2003 following the loss of *Columbia* and the death of all seven astronauts on board.

Below **Atop its shuttle carrier aircraft (SCA), the *Challenger* space shuttle flies over the Johnson Space Center in Houston, Texas, on the way back from its landing site to its launch site.**

Launched in May 1996, the X Prize will be won by the developers of a spacecraft that can carry three people to a height of 62.5 miles (100 km), return safely to Earth, and repeat the feat within two weeks:

The X Prize is a $10,000,000 prize to jumpstart the space tourism industry through competition between the most talented entrepreneurs and rocket experts in the world. . . . For more than thirty years, the general public has waited for an opportunity to enjoy the space frontier on a first-hand basis. The X Prize Foundation is working to make space travel possible for all.

The X Prize Foundation

SPACE STATIONS

A space station is an artificial earth-orbiting satellite that is used as a long-term base for scientific experimentation. The first space station, *Salyut 1*, launched by the Soviet Union in 1971, operated for almost six months. Five more Salyut stations followed. Technology developed during the Salyut program was put to use on *Mir*, launched in 1986.

Assembled in space from several separately launched modules, *Mir* was occupied almost continuously until 2001. *Skylab*, launched by the United States, was used in 1973 and 1974. The *International Space Station (ISS)* is a cooperative project between sixteen countries. The first parts of *ISS* were sent into space on board the space shuttle in 1998, and the first three-person crew took up residence in 2000. At a relatively low altitude of around 240 miles (386 km), *ISS* travels around the earth in around ninety-two minutes.

SEE ALSO
- Armstrong, Neil • Astronauts
- Astronomical Instruments • Astronomy
- Gagarin, Yury • Glenn, John H • NASA • Satellites
- SETI • Shepard, Alan B., Jr. • Solar System
- Space Exploration

SPACE EXPLORATION

THE FIRST JOURNEYS INTO SPACE were carried out in the same spirit of heroism, adventure, and discovery that inspired the great ocean voyages of the fifteenth and sixteenth centuries. Space exploration has given people a new sense of their place in the universe and raises the question of whether humanity will always be bound to the planet Earth. Yet space missions, both manned and unmanned, remain extremely expensive, and though several countries engage in space exploration, most missions are funded and undertaken by the United States.

FIRST STEPS TOWARD THE STARS

The exploration of space by earthbound astronomers dates back many thousands of years. The standard instrument of celestial observation in the ancient and medieval world, the astrolabe, was superseded by the telescope in the seventeenth century. However, it was not until rocket-propulsion technology was developed in the early twentieth century that the notion of an explorer leaving the earth and conducting firsthand exploration of space became a serious consideration.

The first object to be propelled out of the earth's atmosphere was the Soviet satellite *Sputnik 1*, which was launched on October 4, 1957. In January 1958 the United States matched this achievement by launching its own satellite, *Explorer 1*. Twelve months later *Luna I*, an unmanned Soviet space probe, made the first flyby of the moon, and in the same year *Luna 2* crash-landed on the moon's surface. *Luna 3* (also 1959) took the first photographs of the far side of the moon. On April 12, 1961, Yury Gagarin, a cosmonaut (Russian astronaut) became the first person to journey into space.

Right **Apollo 16 commander John W. Young collects samples of moon rock in 1972. At his feet is a gnomon, a device for measuring the sun's altitude.**

Exploring the Moon

With its great rival, the Soviet Union, having seized an early lead in the so-called space race, the United States was determined to be the first nation to put a person on the moon. In preparation for a moon landing, NASA (the National Aeronautics and Space Administration) launched a series of exploratory missions (*Apollo 7, 8, 9,* and *10*). From lunar orbit in 1968, the astronauts of *Apollo 8* became the first humans to observe the far side of the moon and took the first photographs of the earth from space.

A Giant Leap for Mankind

On July 16, 1969, *Apollo 11* blasted off from the Cape Kennedy space center in Florida. Four days later Neil Armstrong and Buzz Aldrin were walking on the moon. People around the world followed the mission on live radio and television broadcasts. Millions witnessed the moment when Neil Armstrong stepped down from the *Eagle* landing module onto the surface of the moon and declared, "that's one small step for [a] man, one giant leap for mankind."

Between November 1969 and December 1972, another five Apollo missions landed on the moon. Astronauts carried out a range of experiments and collected rock and soil samples. Study of moon rocks revealed that, despite its current lifeless state, the moon had had a long history of geological activity.

Above **This photo, taken from the lunar module *Orion* (which casts a shadow in the foreground) shows the lunar roving vehicle (LRV) on its final journey.**

January 2, 1959
Luna 1, the first spacecraft to fly past the moon, is launched.

April 12, 1961
The Russian cosmonaut Yury Gagarin becomes the first person in space.

December 14, 1962
Mariner 2 achieves a flyby of Venus.

July 14, 1965
Mariner 4 becomes the first spacecraft to fly past Mars.

December 24, 1968
Apollo 8 is the first manned spacecraft to orbit the moon.

July 20, 1969
Apollo 11 takes Neil Armstrong and Buzz Aldrin to the surface of the moon.

March 3, 1972
Pioneer 10 is launched on a mission to observe Jupiter.

April 5, 1973
Pioneer 11 is launched on a journey that, six and a half years later, takes it past Saturn.

November 3, 1973
Mariner 10 is launched toward Mercury.

1975
Two Viking spacecraft are sent, with landers on board, to look for signs of life on Mars.

1976
Helios 2 begins collecting solar data.

John W. Young BORN 1930

*W*hereas only a handful of people have journeyed into space even once, the NASA astronaut John Young has traveled beyond the earth's atmosphere six times. Young's first flight was aboard *Gemini 3* in 1965, when he operated the first computer to be used on a manned space flight. He flew again on *Gemini 10* the following year, this time as commander. In 1969 Young was the command module pilot on *Apollo 10,* the last flight before the historic moon landing. Just three years later, aboard *Apollo 16,* he too traveled to the moon.

Then, in 1981, came another groundbreaking achievement: Young was named commander of the first space shuttle flight. On his final flight, in 1983, he commanded the first *Spacelab* mission. On that mission, the space shuttle's cargo bay was used as a mobile space station in which scientists carried out more than seventy experiments across a range of disciplines. In 1996 Young became associate director of the Johnson Space Center in Houston, Texas.

1977
Voyager 1 and *Voyager 2* are launched; their goal is a flyby of Jupiter, Saturn, Uranus, and Neptune and thereafter an exploration of interstellar space.

OCTOBER 18, 1989
Galileo is launched on a journey that, over six years later, takes it into orbit around Jupiter.

NOVEMBER 7, 1996
Mars Global Surveyor is sent to map Mars.

OCTOBER 15, 1997
Cassini is launched toward Saturn.

JANUARY 22, 2003
Pioneer 10 sends its last signal back to Earth from beyond Jupiter.

SEPTEMBER 21, 2003
The *Galileo* mission finally ends as the probe disintegrates in Jupiter's atmosphere.

JANUARY 2004
The Mars exploration rovers *Spirit* and *Opportunity* explore the planet's surface.

MAY 2004
Messenger is launched to study Mercury.

JULY 1, 2004
Cassini reaches Saturn and enters orbit.

Above In 1981 John W. Young commanded the first space shuttle mission aboard *Columbia;* he is pictured here preparing to log data in a flight activities notebook.

DESTINATION: MARS

With the moon landing achieved, the attention of space explorers turned inevitably to Mars, the earth's closest planetary neighbor. The Americans achieved the first Mars flyby in 1965, when *Mariner 4* passed within 6,117 miles (9,844 km) of the red planet and sent back the first close-up images. *Mariners 6* and *7* flew even closer to Mars in 1969 and sent back data that enabled scientists to calculate the exact size and shape of the planet. It was also revealed that Mars has an ice cap, made of carbon dioxide, at its south pole.

After several attempts to launch missions to Mars had ended in failure, in 1971 the Soviet Union succeeded in putting two spacecraft into orbit around the planet. *Mars 2* and *Mars 3* recorded varying surface temperatures that ranged between 55° F (13° C) and 230° F (110° C). They also made relief maps and collected data on the planet's gravitational and magnetic fields.

VIKING INVASION

The first successful landing on Mars took place on July 20, 1976, when the lander released by *Viking 1* touched down. In September the *Viking 2* lander touched down on the opposite side of the planet. Using a range of instruments, the lander took pho-

Right **Viking 1 was launched by a Titan/Centaur rocket from Cape Canaveral Air Force Station in Florida at 5:22 P.M. (EDT) on August 20, 1975, on a half-billion-mile, eleven-month journey to explore Mars. The four-ton (3,629 kg) spacecraft went into orbit around the red planet in mid-1976.**

tographs, gathered data about the atmosphere, and carried out experiments on samples of soil collected with remote-controlled scoops.

Exploring the Planet

It was twenty years before another space probe landed successfully on Mars. With the aid of protective airbags, *Pathfinder* bounced on to the planet's dusty surface in 1997. Data and images sent back by the lander and the roving exploration vehicle, *Sojourner*, indicated that, between 3.5 and 4 billion years ago, Mars may have had large reserves of water (and thus was perhaps capable of supporting life). Evidence from *Mars Global Surveyor (MGS)*, which went into orbit around Mars in 1997, suggested that water might still be present beneath the surface.

Other projects carried out by *MGS* included the production, in 1999, of a topographic map by means of the Mars orbital laser altimeter (MOLA). The map revealed that the northern hemisphere of the planet is significantly lower and smoother than the southern hemisphere, which is scarred with craters.

Late in 2003 no fewer than four spacecraft were heading toward Mars. Two of them, NASA's exploration rovers *Spirit and Opportunity*, landed on opposite sides of the planet in January 2004 and set about on a detailed investigation of Mars's surface.

Reaching Out to the Red Planet

As more is known and understood about Mars, particularly about the existence of water on its surface or underground, the theory that Mars might once have supported life is gaining ground. In 2004 the U.S. president, George W. Bush, announced plans to establish a permanent space station on the moon and suggested that such a structure could act as a launch pad for a manned mission to Mars around 2030.

In 2004 the U.S. president greeted the success of NASA's unmanned Mars exploration missions with a pledge to renew efforts in the manned exploration of space:

Mankind is drawn to the heavens for the same reason we were once drawn into unknown lands and across the open sea. We choose to explore space because doing so improves our lives and lifts our national spirit. . . . The human thirst for knowledge ultimately cannot be satisfied by even the most vivid pictures or the most detailed measurements. We need to see and examine and touch for ourselves, and only human beings are capable of adapting to the inevitable uncertainties posed by space travel.

George W. Bush, January 2004

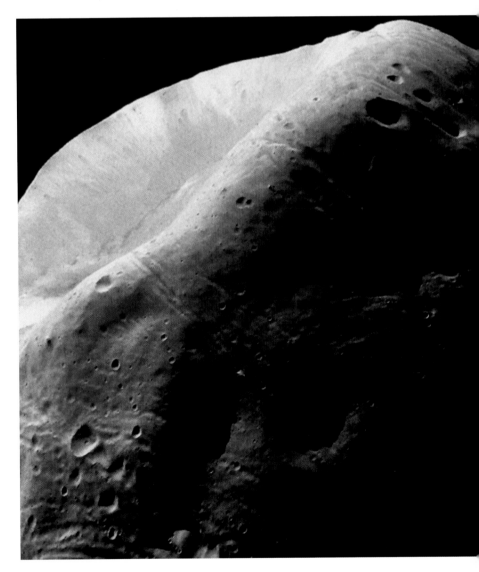

Above **This image of Phobos, the larger of Mars's two moons, was taken by the *Mars Global Surveyor* in 1998. Irregular in shape and heavily cratered, Phobos measures 16.8 miles (27 km) across at its widest point.**

Right **A photograph of one of the Soviet Union's *Venera* Venus space probes.**

EXPLORATION OF THE HOT PLANETS

The first attempts to explore Venus were hampered by its thick layer of acidic cloud and the very high pressure of the planet's atmosphere. Four early *Venera* landers, sent by the Soviet Union, were crushed in the atmosphere before touchdown. Nevertheless, between 1970 and 1981 eight *Venera* craft were landed on Venus. The last Venus mission of the twentieth century was undertaken by *Magellan*, launched by NASA in 1989 and operational until 1994. Using radar technology, *Magellan* mapped the topography of Venus from orbit.

Until 2004 the only mission to have explored Mercury was NASA's *Mariner 10,* which flew by in 1974. Although the images taken by *Mariner 10* are too small for analysis to produce any certain results, scientists believe that much of Mercury's surface was formed by volcanic activity. The *Messenger* probe (*Messenger* is an acronym for *Mercury Surface, Space Environment, Geochemistry* and *Ranging*), launched by the United States in 2004, will begin studying Mercury's mineral composition and general geology from orbit in 2009.

TO JUPITER

NASA's *Pioneer 10,* launched on a mission to Jupiter in March 1972, was the first probe to negotiate the hazardous asteroid belt, a stream of thousands of flying rocks that lies between the orbital paths of Mars and Jupiter. *Pioneer 10* reached Jupiter in December 1973 and sent back to Earth the first close-up images of the giant planet.

Voyager 1 and *Voyager 2,* which flew by Jupiter in 1979, discovered three previously unknown moons. They also observed active volcanoes on the moon Io—the first time any such phenomenon had been observed anywhere in the universe other than Earth. In 1995 a probe launched by the *Galileo* spacecraft descended through the atmosphere of Jupiter and sent back data about the planet's temperature, wind speeds, and pressure. The probe was crushed by the pressure of

Jupiter's atmosphere after less than one hour. Images from *Cassini,* which flew by Jupiter in 2000, revealed more about the complex and violent weather patterns on the planet.

SATURN AND BEYOND

Saturn was visited by a spacecraft for the first time in September 1979, when *Pioneer 11* flew within thirteen thousand miles (21,000 km) of the cloud tops. In 1980 and 1981 the two *Voyager* spacecraft discovered three new moons and observed the spokelike structure of Saturn's rings. *Cassini* arrived at Saturn on July 1, 2004, and began a four-year study of the planet's rings, its weather system, and its thirty-one known moons.

Voyager 2 is the only spacecraft to have reached Uranus and Neptune. Flying past Uranus in 1986, *Voyager 2* photographed the ring system and ten previously undiscovered moons. Reaching Neptune in 1989, the probe observed storms on the planet's surface and discovered six additional moons.

Deep Space Network

*A*n international network of antennas enables continuous communication between space missions and the earth. Operated by NASA, the Deep Space Network, which came into full operation in 1963, eliminates the need for each space mission to set up its own earth communication system. Three complexes are spaced at roughly equal intervals around the world to ensure that, whatever the location of a spacecraft in relation to the spinning Earth, communication is not broken. The complexes, each housing several dish antennas measuring up to 230 feet (70 m) in diameter, are located at Goldstone in the Mojave Desert, California; near Canberra, in southeastern Australia; and near Madrid, in central Spain. Their tasks include transmitting commands, tracking a spacecraft's position and speed, and receiving data.

Below **This image of Saturn was taken by *Pioneer 11* on August 26, 1979, when the probe was 1,768,422 miles (2,846,000 km) from the ringed planet.**

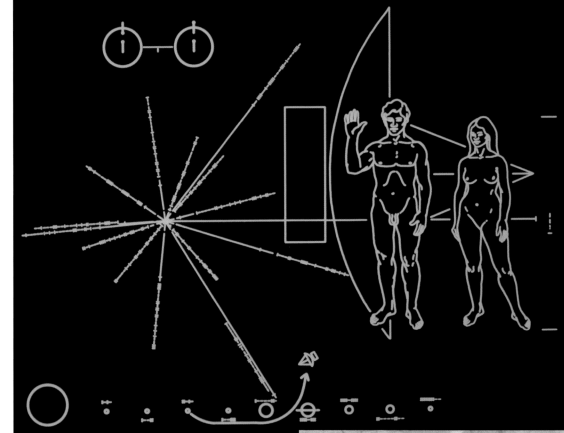

Right **This plaque is attached to the exterior of *Pioneer 10* and *11*. The symbol at top left represents a hydrogen atom. Below, lines radiate from the sun to the relative positions of fourteen pulsars, sources of radio energy. Human figures are set against the spacecraft to give scale. At bottom is a plan of the solar system, showing the route of a *Pioneer* spacecraft from Earth.**

STUDYING THE SUN

In the 1970s NASA developed two unmanned solar probes in cooperation with West German scientists. *Helios 1*, launched in 1974, and *Helios 2*, launched in 1976, collected data about solar wind and solar radiation until 1981. SOHO, the Solar and Heliospheric Observatory (launched in 1995) studies the internal structure of the sun and gathers information about phenomena related to the sun's magnetic field.

THE FINAL FRONTIER

After completing its flyby of Jupiter, *Pioneer 10* flew on into deep space. Its last signal, picked up by the Deep Space Network in 2003, was beamed from 7.8 billion miles (12.6 billion km) away. *Pioneer 11* continued to transmit data until 1995. The two Voyager craft are still transmitting signals from the outer edge of the solar system. In mid-2004 *Voyager 1* was around 8.7 billion miles (14 billion km) from the sun. Some experts believe it is already in the so-called region of termination shock, where the speed of solar wind rapidly slows down. Beyond this zone lies the heliopause, where the influence of the sun is no longer felt. Farther away still lie the mysteries of interstellar space.

Message in a Bottle

*P*ioneers 10 and 11 both carry a plaque engraved with an image of a man and a woman. The plaque also carries scientific data that scientists believe a technologically advanced civilization would be able to interpret. The Voyager spacecraft carry a recording of greetings in fifty-five languages, as well as a variety of earth sounds, such as thunder and birdsong.

SEE ALSO

- Armstrong, Neil • Astronauts
- Astronomical Instruments • Astronomy
- Gagarin, Yury • Glenn, John H. • NASA • Satellites
- SETI • Shepard, Alan B., Jr. • Solar System
- Spacecraft

SPAIN

FROM THE LATE FIFTEENTH CENTURY to the mid-seventeenth, Spain led the European exploration and conquest of Central and South America. Spain's total domination of the New World had an immeasurable and lasting impact on the region's culture, religion, language, economy, and social and political structures. Spain's vast overseas empire brought the country unprecedented wealth and significantly affected the balance of power within Europe.

NATURAL ADVANTAGES

The geographical position of Spain and Portugal within Europe made them an obvious starting point for transatlantic navigation and gave the two countries a significant head start in exploration to the west. Not only do Spain and Portugal border on the ocean, but they are also within easy sailing distance of the Canary Islands, a highly useful staging post that came into Spanish hands in 1480. Moreover, the sweep of ocean currents and the direction of prevailing winds make crossing the Atlantic much easier from Spain and Portugal than from countries farther north. Many Spanish fishermen and merchants had gained experience of ocean sailing in their daily work.

STRENGTH THROUGH UNITY

Geographical position and maritime experience would have mattered little, however, if other conditions within Spain had not also been favorable for exploration and conquest. Political unity, a crucial factor, was achieved in 1469 with the marriage of Isabella of Castile and Ferdinand of Aragon, the heirs of Spain's two most powerful kingdoms. Internal Spanish power was greatly strengthened in

Left **John II, king of Castile, begins his defeat of the Moors at the Battle of Higueruela (1431) as the centuries-long struggle to drive the Muslims out of Spain enters its final phase.**

Above **This eighteenth-century Spanish painting depicts Diego Velázquez giving Hernán Cortés command of an expedition (1519–1521) to conquer the Aztecs. Cortés added the colony of New Spain (Mexico) to Spain's possessions.**

peoples who, it seemed, would offer little in terms of military resistance. The Treaty of Tordesillas, ratified in 1494, gave Spain possession of all new discoveries west of an imaginary line 370 leagues (around 1,100 miles, or 1,775 km) west of the Cape Verde Islands. Spain's rivals, the Portuguese, could claim possession of lands east of the line.

A RESERVOIR OF TALENT

The conclusion of the *Reconquista* had left Spain with an army but no war to fight. The New World offered scores of young soldiers an ideal outlet for their energies. In the twenty years following Columbus's last voyage (1502–1503), numerous Spanish voyages searched the coasts of northern and eastern South America for pearls, gold, and other riches. Notable voyages were led by Juan Ponce de León, who became the first governor of Puerto Rico in 1509, and Sebastián de Belalcázar, who took part in the conquest of Nicaragua.

THE VAST PACIFIC

While the exploration and settlement of Central America was under way, the true goal of Spanish efforts remained a westerly route to Southeast Asia. When Vasco Núñez de Balboa crossed Panama in 1513 and came upon the Pacific Ocean, the prized Spice Islands seemed tantalizingly close.

In 1519 and 1520 Ferdinand Magellan sailed down the Atlantic coast of South America in search of a passage to the Pacific.

1492 with the successful conclusion of the *Reconquista,* the expulsion from the Iberian Peninsula of the Muslims who had held large areas of it since the eighth century. Later the same year, Christopher Columbus set off on his first journey west across the Atlantic, buoyed by the hopes of a confident nation.

A NEW EMPIRE

Columbus's journey demonstrated that by sailing west it was possible to reach unexplored lands that might contain great wealth. Moreover, the lands were inhabited by native

Accepting the surrender of Atahualpa, Francisco Pizarro addressed the defeated Incan king as follows:

Do not take it as an insult that you have been defeated . . . for I have conquered greater kingdoms than yours, and have defeated other more powerful lords than you, imposing on them the dominion of the Emperor, whose vassal [servant] I am, and who is King of Spain and of the universal world. We come to conquer this land by his command, that all may come to acknowledge of God, and of his Holy Catholic Faith.

Quoted in C. H. Markham, ed., *Reports on the Discovery of Peru* (1872)

He almost reached the continent's southernmost extent before negotiating a route through the strait now named after him. His crossing of the Pacific revealed for the first time the vast extent of that ocean (greatly underestimated until then) and the difficulty of reaching Asia by sailing west from Europe.

New Spain and South America

Meanwhile, between 1519 and 1521 Hernán Cortés's conquest of the Aztec Empire added the colony of New Spain (present-day Mexico) to the Spanish Empire. From Panama, Francisco Pizarro launched three expeditions southward along the Pacific coast of South America. In 1533, having crossed the Andes, his army took possession of the Incan Empire. Much of present-day Peru, Ecuador, Bolivia, and Chile fell under Spanish control.

Below **A sixteenth-century impression of the extraordinary conquest of the Incan Empire by a small force of Spaniards led by Francisco Pizarro.**

Disease

The relative ease with which the Spanish conquered the native peoples of South and Central America was as much the result of disease as superior weaponry. Half the population of the Aztec capital, Tenochtitlán, was infected with smallpox by the time Cortés entered the city in 1520. A smallpox epidemic also contributed to the collapse of the Incan Empire between 1527 and 1530. Experts estimate that by 1595 more than 18 million Native Americans had died from smallpox, cholera, typhus, and measles—diseases they had no experience of and thus no immunity to.

THE IMPACT OF SPANISH EXPANSION

The Spanish conquest of Central and South America made a lasting difference to the racial, cultural, linguistic, and religious character of the region. While many Spaniards argued that indigenous peoples should be treated with moderation and respect, the conquistadores' desire to spread Christianity, to win new territory, and to gain wealth all too often degenerated into cruel treatment of native peoples.

During the sixteenth century Spain's power and influence were fed by the gold and silver that poured in from the Americas. Much of the wealth, however, was spent on wars with the Netherlands, France, and England (the poorly planned and never-executed Enterprise of England, which was supposed to involve the use of the ill-fated Spanish Armada to ferry the Duke of Parma's army of invasion from the Dutch coast in 1588, was terribly wasteful of wealth, ships, and lives). Imported riches masked the decline in the economy within Spain. When the influx of silver slowed, Spain's age of greatness came to an end.

SEE ALSO

- Belalcázar, Sebastián de
- Colonization and Conquest
- Columbian Exchange • Columbus, Christopher
- Cortés, Hernán • Ferdinand and Isabella
- Magellan, Ferdinand • Narváez, Pánfilo de
- Núñez de Balboa, Vasco • Pinzón, Martín Alonso
- Pinzón, Vicente Yáñez • Ponce de León, Juan
- Soto, Hernando de • Vespucci, Amerigo

Below **After two years' preparation, the formidable Spanish Armada, the subject of this painting, was launched in 1588 as part of an attempted conquest of Britain. It was defeated by a British fleet led by Lord Charles Howard and Sir Francis Drake.**

SPEKE, JOHN HANNING

AN ENGLISH EXPLORER AND SOLDIER, John Hanning Speke (1827–1864) joined Richard Francis Burton's expeditions to East Africa in the 1850s. Burton and Speke's aim was to discover the source of the Nile River. Speke's correct identification of the river's principal source—Lake Victoria—led to a bitter dispute with Burton. Speke died in tragic circumstances before the accuracy of his claim was generally accepted.

Below **A contemporary portrait of John Hanning Speke, discoverer of the source of the Nile.**

SPEKE THE SOLDIER

The youngest son of wealthy parents, John Hanning Speke was born in Ilminster, southwestern England, on May 4, 1827. In 1844, when Speke was seventeen, he joined the Indian army, the British colonial force in India. It was while serving in India that Speke became interested in travel and exploration. During periods of leave, he went on hunting expeditions with James Augustus Grant (1827–1892), a fellow army officer. The two men advanced far into the Himalayas and crossed the frontier into Tibet, a territory that was generally closed off to Europeans.

TEAMING UP WITH BURTON

Speke's African adventures began in 1854, when he teamed up with Richard Francis Burton (1821–1890), who, like himself, was an officer in the Indian army. Burton had been asked by the army to explore Somaliland in the Horn of Africa (a region that includes present-day Ethiopia, Somalia, and Djibouti).

In April 1855 the expedition was attacked by Somalis. Burton got away, but Speke was captured and wounded. He later escaped and returned to England to recover. In 1856 he served in the last months of the Crimean War (1854–1856), in which the British supported the resistance of the Turkish Ottoman Empire to Russian expansion into the Crimea (part of present-day Ukraine).

SEARCH FOR THE SOURCE OF THE NILE

In 1856 Burton was invited by London's Royal Geographical Society to lead an expedition to Africa. He was given the task of exploring the Great Lakes of East Africa and of establishing which of them, if any, was the source of the Nile River. A mystery that had occupied geographers since ancient times, the location of the source of the Nile was one of the most sought-after prizes of nineteenth-century exploration. Burton asked Speke to join him in his quest.

In August 1857 Burton and Speke headed inland from their starting point on the eastern coast of Africa. On February 13, 1858, after traveling some 745 miles (1,200 km), they reached a great lake, known locally as the Sea of Ujiji (the lake's present-day name is Lake Tanganyika). Although ill health thwarted the two men's attempts to conduct a full exploration of the Sea of Ujiji, Speke managed to explore parts of it by canoe. Having done so, Speke concluded that Lake Tanganyika could not be the source of the Nile. Burton, on the other hand, became convinced that it was.

SPEKE REACHES LAKE VICTORIA

On the return journey to the coast, Speke and Burton split up. While Speke headed north to investigate another lake he had heard reports of, Burton, too ill to make the journey, waited at Kezeh (present-day Tabora, in Tanzania). On August 3, 1858, Speke reached the lake, known as Ukerewe to Africans. He named it Lake Victoria, in honor of the reigning Queen of England. Although he did not make a full survey of the lake, Speke was struck by its great size (it is Africa's largest lake). He decided that Lake Victoria must be the source of the Nile River.

Back in Kezeh, Speke told Burton of his discovery. Burton's refusal to accept that Speke had found the Nile's source marked the start of a long-running disagreement between the two explorers. However, as neither Lake Tanganyika nor Lake Victoria had been com-

Right **Although Speke discovered the source of the Nile in 1862 (and thus settled a question that had dominated nineteenth-century exploration of East Africa), the controversy continued until 1875, when Henry Morton Stanley finally proved the accuracy of Speke's discovery.**

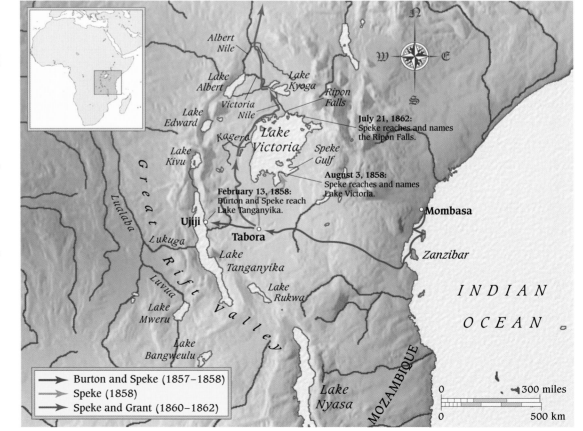

The Nile River

*T*he Nile is the longest river in the world. From source to sea it is 4,160 miles (6,695 km) long. It flows north out of Lake Victoria and through a series of deep gorges before widening out across a large swamp of papyrus reeds, called the Sudd, in Sudan. At this point it becomes the White Nile and is joined by the Blue Nile and the Atbara River, both of which start in the highlands of Ethiopia. The river then meanders across its floodplain in Egypt. North of Cairo, the Egyptian capital, it slows and divides as it opens into a huge delta some 155 miles (250 km) wide before it finally reaches the Mediterranean Sea.

pletely explored, the mystery could be resolved only with further investigation. In 1860 the Royal Geographical Society sent Speke, accompanied by his old comrade James Augustus Grant, back to Africa to survey Lake Victoria.

"THE NILE IS SETTLED"

On July 21, 1862, Speke and Grant located a waterfall (the Ripon Falls) at the northern end of Lake Victoria that emptied into a river flowing north. Following the river down-

Left **This sketch map of the East African Great Lakes region was drawn by Speke in 1857 or 1858.**

MAY 4, 1827
John Hanning Speke is born in Ilminster, England.

1844–1849
Serves with the British army in India; explores the Himalayas and Tibet with James Augustus Grant.

1854–1855
Joins Richard Francis Burton's expedition to Somaliland.

1856
Serves with the British army during the Crimean War.

1857–1858
Explores the Great Lakes of East Africa with Burton.

1862
Returning to Lake Victoria, discovers it to be the primary source of the Nile River.

SEPTEMBER 15, 1864
Dies in a shooting accident in England.

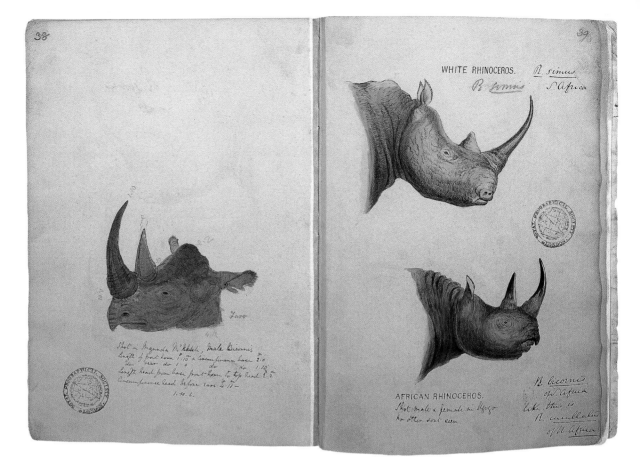

WHITE RHINOCEROS.

AFRICAN RHINOCEROS.

Above **Speke's records of the wildlife he encountered during his African journeys include these sketches of a white rhinoceros.**

Speke described his sense of elation at discovering the source of the Nile:

Here at last I stood on the brink of the Nile; most beautiful was the scene, nothing could surpass it! It was . . . a magnificent stream from 600 to 700 yards wide, dotted with islets and rocks, the former occupied with fishermen's huts, the latter by sterns and crocodiles basking in the sun. . . . Herds of the nsunnu [antelope] and hartebeest could be seen grazing, while the hippopotami were snorting in the water.

John Hanning Speke, *Journal of the Discovery of the Source of the Nile* (1863)

stream through present-day Uganda, they entered Sudan, where they met the English explorer Samuel Baker and his wife, Florence, traveling in the opposite direction. The Bakers told Speke that they had traveled upstream from Egypt on their own quest to find the source of the Nile. With this encounter Speke was certain that he had succeeded in tracing the source of the mighty river. He sent a cable home, with the message "the Nile is settled."

A Tragic End

Burton continued to insist that he, and not Speke, had been the first to identify the source of the Nile. Just before a planned public debate of the issue with Burton, Speke shot himself dead in a hunting accident (some suspected that the incident was no accident but an admission of error by Speke). The Nile controversy was finally settled in the 1870s, when the explorations of David Livingstone and Henry Morton Stanley proved Speke's theory correct.

SEE ALSO

- Burton, Richard Francis • Livingstone, David
- Stanley, Henry Morton
- Tinné, Alexandrine-Pieternella-Françoise

STANLEY, HENRY MORTON

HENRY MORTON STANLEY (1841–1904) was born in Wales and settled in the United States at an early age. In 1869, while working as a journalist, he was sent to find the Scottish explorer David Livingstone, who was missing in East Africa. Stanley's search ended in a famous meeting between the two men in 1871. After exploring regions of eastern and central Africa, Stanley won a large colony for Belgium. His expedition along the Congo River is one of the great achievements of nineteenth-century exploration.

Below **Henry Morton Stanley was known for his strong will, independence, and determination.**

A CHANGE OF NAME

The man who was to gain fame as Henry Morton Stanley was born John Rowlands in the small town of Denbigh in northern Wales in 1841. Raised from the age of six in a poorhouse (a charitable institution), he received only a basic education. In 1859 he ran away to sea and sailed to America as a cabin boy. He jumped ship at New Orleans and was taken in by Henry Hope Stanley, a merchant. John changed his own name to Henry Stanley, in honor of the man who had given him home and shelter, and later added the middle name Morton.

"FIND LIVINGSTONE"

After serving in the American Civil War (1861–1865), Stanley worked as a war correspondent for the *New York Herald*. In 1868 he was sent to the East African country of Abyssinia (present-day Ethiopia). In 1869, while reporting on a revolution in Spain, he was given an assignment that changed his life.

Stanley received instructions from James Gordon Bennett, the owner of the *New York Herald,* to "find Livingstone." The man in question was David Livingstone, a Scottish missionary and explorer who had disappeared in East Africa while searching for the source of the Nile River. Nothing had been heard from Livingstone for three years.

H. M. STANLEY,
from a Photograph taken at Simon's Town, Cape of Good Hope,
soon after emerging from Africa (on the West Coast) May 1877

THROUGH THE DARK CONTINENT

OR

THE SOURCES OF THE NILE
AROUND THE GREAT LAKES OF EQUATORIAL AFRICA
AND DOWN THE LIVINGSTONE RIVER
TO THE ATLANTIC OCEAN

BY

HENRY M. STANLEY

AUTHOR OF "HOW I FOUND LIVINGSTONE," "COOMASSIE AND MAGDALA,"
"MY KALULU," ETC

IN TWO VOLUMES
VOL. II

MAPS AND ILLUSTRATIONS

LONDON
SAMPSON LOW, MARSTON, SEARLE & RIVINGTON
CROWN BUILDINGS, 188 FLEET STREET
1878

[All rights reserved]

THE SEARCH BEGINS

Stanley did not begin his search immediately. Instead, he traveled to Egypt, where he reported on the opening of the Suez Canal (on November 17, 1869). He continued to the Crimea (a Black Sea region of present-day Ukraine), Persia (present-day Iran), and India. In January 1871 he arrived at Zanzibar, an island off the eastern coast of Africa. There Arab slave traders told him that a white man fitting Livingstone's description was living at the village of Ujiji, on the shore of Lake Tanganyika. Stanley gathered together a team of porters and pack animals, and in March 1871 the search party left Bagamoyo (in present-day Tanzania) and headed west toward Ujiji.

LIVINGSTONE LOCATED

Stanley found Livingstone at Ujiji on November 10, 1871, and later described the moment of their famous meeting in a best-selling book. Livingstone did not in fact regard himself as lost—he explained that he was merely resting while he recovered from illness. The two men became friends, and Livingstone encouraged Stanley to take an interest in exploration.

JANUARY 29, 1841
Henry Morton Stanley is born John Rowlands in northern Wales.

1856
Begins work, first for a haberdasher and then for a butcher.

1859
Arrives in New Orleans; changes name to Henry Stanley.

1861–1865
Enlists in the Confederate Army during the American Civil War and then changes sides and serves as a Union seaman.

1865
Becomes a journalist.

1869
Is asked by the *New York Herald* to search East Africa for the missing explorer David Livingstone.

1871
Meets David Livingstone at Ujiji; together the men explore the northern end of Lake Tanganyika.

Stanley describes his meeting with David Livingstone in this memorable excerpt:

So I did that which I thought was most dignified. I pushed back the crowds, and, passing from the rear, walked down a living avenue of people, until I came in front of the semicircle of Arabs, in the front of which stood the white man with the grey beard. As I advanced slowly towards him I noticed he was pale, looked wearied, had a grey beard, wore a bluish cap with a faded gold band round it, had on a red-sleeved waistcoat, and a pair of grey tweed trousers. I would have run to him, only I was a coward in the presence of such a mob—would have embraced him, only, he being an Englishman, I did not know how he would receive me; so I did what cowardice and false pride suggested was the best thing—walked deliberately to him, took off my hat, and said:

"Dr Livingstone, I presume?"

"Yes," said he, with a kind smile, lifting his hat slightly.

H. M. Stanley, *How I Found Livingstone* (1872)

STANLEY THE EXPLORER

When Stanley arrived in England, he was greeted as a national hero and awarded a medal by the Royal Geographical Society. In 1873, following the death of Livingstone in Africa, Stanley decided to devote himself to the exploration of the great continent.

Above **A posed studio photograph of Henry Morton Stanley in the clothing he wore during his African expeditions.**

1874–1877
Stanley circumnavigates Lakes Victoria and Tanganyika and explores the Lualaba and Congo Rivers. Completes the crossing of central Africa from east to west.

1879–1884
Wins the Congo for Belgium; explores Lakes Tumba and Leopold II.

1887–1889
Leads Emin Pasa Relief Expedition; explores Semliki River and Ruwenzori Mountains.

1895–1900
Serves as a member of Parliament; receives a knighthood from Queen Victoria.

MAY 10, 1904
Dies in England.

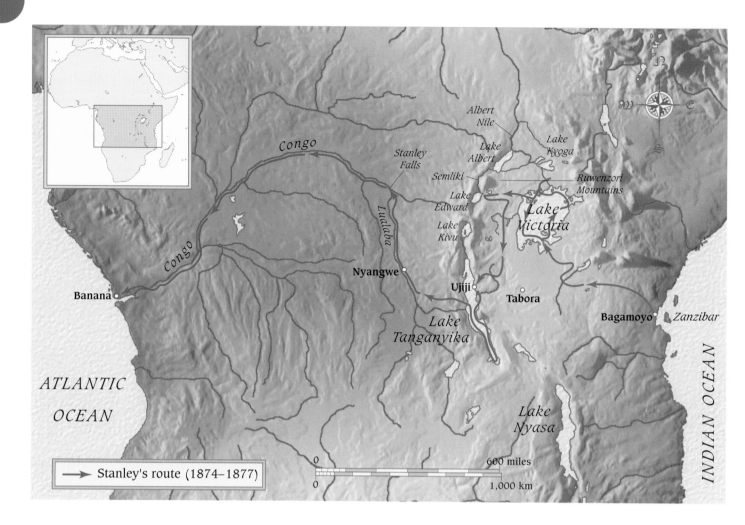

Stanley's route (1874–1877)

Above **Stanley's east-west crossing of Africa (1874–1877), an epic journey across extremely hazardous territory, answered fundamental questions about the nature and course of the Nile and the Congo, Africa's mightiest rivers.**

In the capacity of correspondent for both the *New York Herald* and the *Daily Telegraph* of London, Stanley set out from Bagamoyo in November 1874 at the head of an expedition of 356 people. The plan was to explore Lake Victoria, which the English explorer John Hanning Speke found in 1858, and to resolve the long-standing dispute over whether that lake really was, as Speke had claimed, the source of the Nile River. Stanley circumnavigated Lake Victoria in February 1875 in the *Lady Alice*, a steamboat that could be divided into sections and carried overland by the expedition's porters. Stanley's journey around Africa's largest lake confirmed that it was indeed the major source of the Nile.

STANLEY EXPLORES THE CONGO

A second aim of Stanley's expedition was to trace the route of the Lualaba River, which flowed north from Lake Tanganyika and thus appeared to be a strong candidate for a source of the Nile. However, after following its initial course, Stanley found that the Lualaba turned west and then southwest in a giant arc and flowed not to the Mediterranean but to the Atlantic, where it was recognized as the Congo River.

Stanley's journey down the river, from its source at Lake Tanganyika to its mouth at Banana, lasted 999 days and has been called "one of the worst journeys in the history of exploration." The *Lady Alice* and twenty-two canoes began the hazardous trip down-stream, but time and again the boats had to be hauled from the water and carried around waterfalls and impassable rapids. Local people attacked the expedition, and Frank Pocock, a companion of Stanley's, drowned. Of the 356 people who had departed Bagamoyo, only

114 reached Banana on August 9, 1877. Stanley's hair had turned white during the journey across the African continent. Yet, however grueling, Stanley's expedition was a pioneering act of exploration.

FINAL AFRICAN EXPEDITION

In 1887 Stanley led a seven-hundred-strong force to the southern Sudan on a mission to rescue Emin Pasa, the German-born governor of the Egyptian Sudan, who had been captured by rebels. After attaining this goal in 1888, Stanley went on to explore the Semliki River in central Africa. His sighting of the Ruwenzori Mountains (between present-day Uganda and the Democratic Republic of Congo) confirmed the accuracy of the description written by the Greek geographer Claudius Ptolemy in the second century CE. Ptolemy had described snow-capped mountains near the equator in Africa and named them *Lunae Montes* (Mountains of the Moon).

Stanley the Colonialist

Stanley's exploration of the Congo (1874–1877) came to the attention of King Leopold II of Belgium (reigned 1865–1909). Leopold commissioned Stanley to win the trust of the native peoples of the region in order that the king might exercise more control over them. One of Stanley's methods of gaining influence was to attach to his hand a buzzer that was connected to a battery. When he shook hands with a chief, the chief received a mild electric shock. This experience served to convince many that Stanley had superhuman powers. Belgium's colonial project was successful, and Leopold II was officially recognized as autonomous sovereign of the Congo Free State in 1885.

Until Stanley saw the Ruwenzori Mountains, few people had believed Ptolemy's account to be true.

Stanley's final years were spent in England, where he served as a member of Parliament (1895–1900). In 1899 he received a knighthood from Queen Victoria, after which he was known as Sir Henry Stanley. He died in 1904.

Left **The Emin Pasa Relief Expedition was one of the best-equipped expeditions ever to travel to Africa. Among the officers selected by Stanley (seated, center) were, from left to right, Thomas Heazle Parke, R. H. Nelson, William G. Stairs, and A. J. Mounteney-Jephson.**

SEE ALSO

- Burton, Richard Francis
- Livingstone, David
- Ptolemy
- Speke, John Hanning

STRABO

IN THE EARLY YEARS of the first century CE, the Greek geographer, historian, and philosopher Strabo (c. 64 BCE–c. 20 CE) compiled his *Geography*, a book based partly on his own travels and partly on the work of others. The *Geography* is a monumental gathering of information about the world known to the people of ancient Rome and Greece and stands as the most important geographical work to have survived from that era.

STRABO THE TRAVELER

It was not uncommon in the ancient Roman world for a person to be given a nickname on the basis of physical appearance. In some instances the person's family name has been forgotten, and the nickname is all that has survived. So it is with Strabo, whose real name is not known but whose nickname derives from the Greek word *strabos,* which means "squint-eyed."

Strabo was born sometime around 64 BCE in the Greek-speaking city of Amaseia (present-day Amasya), on the Black Sea coast of the Anatolian Peninsula (now northern Turkey). Early in life Strabo left Amaseia and went to Rome, where he was taught grammar and philosophy by leading scholars. He traveled west as far as Tuscany in Italy and east into Armenia, a land that lies between the Black Sea and the Caspian Sea. He crossed the Mediterranean Sea to the Egyptian city of Alexandria, the center of Greek and Roman learning. From Alexandria he journeyed up the Nile as far as the first cataract (an impass-

able waterfall), near present-day Aswan. Eventually Strabo returned to Rome, where he devoted himself to writing.

STRABO THE WRITER

Strabo wrote two major works. His first, a history of Greece and Rome, survives only in fragments quoted by other ancient writers. His second survives almost intact. Called

c. 64 BCE
Strabo is born at Amaseia, in northern Anatolia.

c. 30s BCE
Travels in western Asia, Europe, and North Africa.

c. 25–24 BCE
Stays in Egypt and explores the Nile River.

c. 18 CE
Completes the writing of *Geography* while in Rome.

c. 20 CE
Dies, possibly at Amaseia.

The Voyage of Pytheas

Strabo's *Geography* refers to a voyage made by Pytheas around 300 BCE. Pytheas claimed to have sailed west from Massalia (Marseilles) in southern France, around the Atlantic coast of Spain and France, and then around Britain. He described Thule, an island that lay six days' sail from Britain and extended north to the Arctic Circle. The region he visited is probably present-day Iceland or Norway.

Pytheas's own account of his voyage, *About the Ocean,* has not survived. Strabo was not alone among ancient writers in the doubt he cast on Pytheas's report (he even condemned Pytheas as an "utter liar"). However, it is now generally accepted that Pytheas did make the journey. Despite Strabo's scepticism, it is thanks to him that a record of Pytheas's journey survives at all.

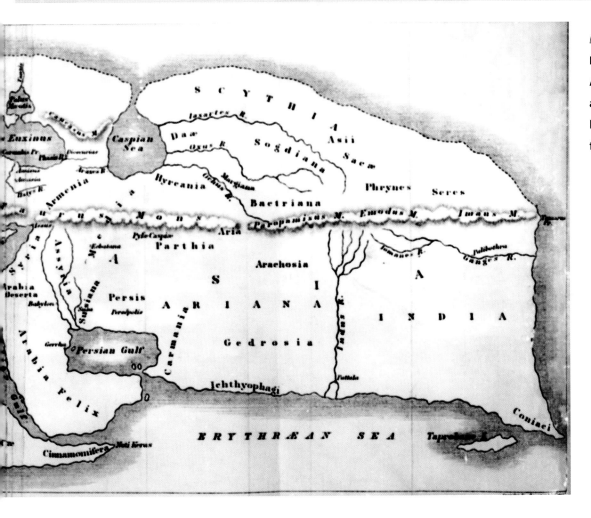

Left **This map of Europe, Asia, and Africa—the world according to Strabo— has been reconstructed from Strabo's writings.**

Geography, it is a mixture of Strabo's own travel records and the work of many other writers whose books he consulted, probably at the great library of Alexandria.

Completed in Rome by about 18 CE, Strabo's *Geography* is divided into seventeen books: two introductory books define the science of geography, eight are about Europe, six about Asia, and one about Africa, mainly Egypt. Written for use by officials, the *Geography* records the names of peoples and cities throughout the Roman world, their customs, the location of harbors, relative distances between given points, the course of rivers, the sites of natural resources, and a good deal more information. For those engaged in the business of government, such data were invaluable.

In his description of the British Isles, Strabo cast doubts on the claims made by Pytheas of Massalia that he had reached an island named Thule:

Brettanike [Britain] is triangular in shape and its longest side stretches beside Gaul [France and Belgium]. . . . There are four crossings which men customarily use from the continent to the island, from the Rhine, from the Seine, from the Loire and from the Garonne. . . . Concerning Thule our information is uncertain, because of its remoteness, the furthest north of all named islands. The things which Pytheas said about this and other places were fabricated, so he is clearly lying. . . .

Strabo, *Geography*, book 4

THE IMPORTANCE OF STRABO'S *GEOGRAPHY*

Strabo's *Geography* was in many respects imperfect. He recorded as history events that are now regarded as mythical—for example, he accepted as fact the journeys of the Greek hero Heracles (Hercules). On the other hand, he rejected texts that had a basis in historical fact, including the work of the historian Herodotus (c. 485–420 BCE), whose books were based on firsthand experience of travel in foreign lands. Likewise, Strabo dismissed the account of the Greek navigator Pytheas of Massalia, who in the fourth century BCE was almost certainly the first Greek to visit and describe the British Isles.

Nevertheless, by assembling a wealth of information into a single work, Strabo created the ancient world's most extensive study of geographical knowledge until it was superseded in the second century CE by Ptolemy's *Geography,* another compendium of ancient geographical knowledge. Strabo's work remained influential for centuries. His

Above **Other than the squint that is suggested by his name, details of Strabo's appearance are a matter of pure conjecture.**

theory, for example, that the Far East could be reached by sailing west from Europe, was shared almost 1,500 years later by Christopher Columbus, whose 1492 journey across the Atlantic proved Strabo right.

SEE ALSO
- Eratosthenes of Cyrene
- Geography
- Ptolemy

GLOSSARY

aft At or near the stern (rear) of a ship.

asteroid A small celestial body, usually a piece of rock.

asteroid belt A region of space between the orbits of Mars and Jupiter where large numbers of asteroids are found.

carvel-built Referring to the hull of a ship constructed by fitting planks to a preconstructed frame and making the surface level by caulking the gaps.

caulk To stop and make watertight, for example, the gaps between the planks of a ship or cracks in a window frame.

clinker-built Referring to the hull of a ship constructed of overlapping planks.

cog A clinker-built, square-rigged, wide transport ship of the Middle Ages, the first to include a rudder in place of a steering oar.

Comanche A member of a Native American people who lived by raiding and hunting buffalo on the southern Great Plains.

comet A celestial body that follows a highly eccentric orbit around the sun; many comets trail a tail of dust behind them when they near the sun.

corona The outermost part of a sun's atmosphere.

delta An often triangular area at the mouth of a river, where the sediment (rocks, gravel, and other material carried by the current) laid down has caused the river to split into channels.

fore At or near the front of a ship.

galleon A large wooden sailing ship used for warfare and commerce, especially by the Spanish during the fifteenth and sixteenth centuries.

gravity The fundamental physical force that one object exerts on another. The size of an object is the primary factor governing the gravitational force it exerts.

greenhouse effect The rise in temperature of the surface and lower atmosphere of the earth or another planet caused by a high presence in the atmosphere of carbon dioxide, which traps reflected heat.

Iberian Peninsula The southwestern part of the European landmass that includes Spain and Portugal.

Inca A member of a people who ruled a large empire in northwestern South America from the thirteenth century until the sixteenth, when it fell to the Spanish conquistadores.

Inca Road The main north-south highway of the Incan Empire, which stretches some 4,350 miles (7,000 km) from Colombia to Chile and clings to the side of the Andes range at altitudes between 3,300 and 14,750 feet (1,000–4,500 m).

keel The V-shaped backbone of a ship.

lateen A rig with a triangular sail hung from a yard fixed diagonally to the mast.

monsoon A wind in southern Asia that blows from the northeast in winter and from the southwest in summer, when it is accompanied by heavy rains.

mountain man A man who worked as a hunter and trapper in the Rocky Mountains in the first half of the nineteenth century, before American settlers moved into the West.

prevailing wind The wind that predominates in a given area or at a given time.

propeller A spiral-shaped shaft driven by the engine to power a ship forward.

solar flare A sudden and intense burst of radioactive energy from a small area of the sun's surface.

solar wind The flow of radioactive particles from the sun.

spar Any of the tapered wooden poles used in the rigging of sails.

sunspot An area of the sun's surface, one associated with strong magnetic activity, that appears darker because it is cooler than the surrounding area.

tack To direct a ship into the wind along a zigzagging course by repeatedly adjusting the direction of the bow and the angle of the sails.

yard A spar crossing the mast to which sails are fixed.

INDEX